JOIN THE
ALLITERATI

the best fresh talent in art and literature

The Lilliput
Shelley Day Sclater

My grandfather, sitting in his wingback chair, rasps his breaths; bare veiny feet in misshapen faded green corduroy slippers rest on the brown tiled hearth. The fire cracks and sputters. My grandmother, in her paisley wrap-around housecoat, comes in and dusts the mantelpiece; she lifts the ornaments one by one, rubs them with the yellow duster, and puts them back. She's already done the brasses. She says: *They've given us that blummen cheap coal again. He shouldn't be sitting up so close but there's No Telling Some Folk. He'll know about it when a spark lands.* She shakes the last of the coals onto the fire and goes out taking the empty scuttle with her. Thick brown smoke hisses up the chimney through a layer of powdery black slack.

In the room – it's not the front room or the living room, it's just *the* room – the smell of coal smoke, brass polish, laundry. Mist on the insides of the windows; outside, rain. The back kitchen door is open; the boiler gulps out great clouds of steam as my grandmother lifts the lid with a folded teatowel and, leaning back, prods at the contents with wooden tongs held the full length of her arm.

My sister and me, in shorts, kneeling up at the table: Lakeland crayons – new ones in little packs of five, plastic press-studded pouches that smell like custard – colouring books, magic painting, thin thin paintbrushes, water in an egg-cup shaped like a shoe. My grandfather says, *Howway bonnie lass, pass is me coupon over, help is fill it in.* Time to do the Pools, win some money. I have to fill it in because Nanna has given up long since and you daren't ask our Derek and my sister's far too young.

I've finished my magic painting anyway. I hold it up to look, blow on it, shake it a bit to make it dry. It's a donkey, standing in a field with some daffodils that have come out brown. The paper's gone lumpy. I kneel up and sing a wee song we learned at school: *Daffodil shiny peep through the green, prettier lady never was seen …* My sister, looking up at my picture, sucking at the bristles on the end of her paintbrush.

My grandfather leans forward, lifts his arm and prods his bony finger in the direction of the football coupon. He said that finger came from the war. Nanna says baloney, he never went near any blinking war. *Howway lass …* he starts, but his words dissolve into coughing. He rests one hand on the mantelpiece and the other on his knee and he coughs and coughs till he retches up with it then spits into the fire and wipes his mouth on his hanky. I lay my picture down carefully away from my sister and stand on my chair to reach the *Vernon's* from off the top of the china cabinet. My grandmother puts her head round the door and looks at my grandfather then at me. I'm not supposed to get him agitated. *Mind ye divvent fall*, she says, then shakes her head and disappears into the back kitchen. My grandfather is just wheezing now, getting his breath. His fingers scrabble in his cardy pocket, feeling for the biro.

The best thing my grandfather likes is his pools. I get to fill it in with tiny little crosses in tiny little squares. He says you can tell I won the prize for neat writing (I had to copy out 'This Royal Throne of Kings' in actual ink). You have to be exact and you don't get a second chance. That's what my grandfather tells me: in the important things, there are No Second Chances. He says, now mind you remember that, bonnie lass.

If you win the pools you get loads of money. Enough to buy Nanna a holiday and me a typewriter. I printed an entire story with my *John Bull* which took for ever and Granda said the lassie needs a typewriter, that's what she needs. We saw a child's one, a Lilliput, in Sheena Robson's catalogue but it was too much. Unless, he said, unless we win the pools, and he tapped the side of his nose with his war finger and winked at me. Nanna was sitting in the other chair, darning. She wound the strand of wool round her finger and snapped it, then looked up, and shook her head. Then she put her work away in the basket and got up to do the tea.

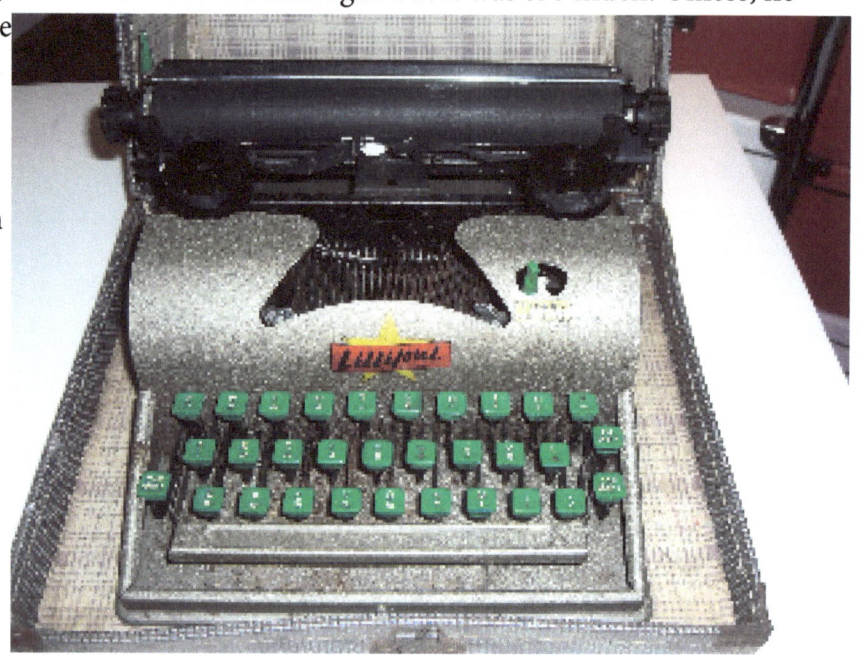

That day I filled out the coupon double quick because Davy next door came knocking for the money. On Saturday I wasn't there for the checking because I was away up the gull ponds with Rosemary Patterson. We'd come back late because we'd seen a dead sheep floating in the rushes, its belly all swollen and its legs sticking up stiff in the air and the smell of it had knocked us sick. When I came flying in the door my grandmother was there in the back kitchen. She said *hey, steady on now* and went on prodding at stock which happened to be a sheep's head boiling with peelings and barley and I felt even sicker at the sight of it. *Get away with you,* she said, laughing. Then she said, *Your granda's won the pools,* and stirred again at the stock. *Go on,* she said, *ask him,* and laughed some more.

I clean forgot about the dead sheep because I was so excited. I ran straight next door to get Sheena Robson's *Grafton's*. She couldn't believe it and had to come into ours to verify while Davy washed his hands from cleaning out the ferrets and came in too. A typewriter was ordered and Mrs R said you could pay it off week by week but there'd be no need for that in this case, would there; she laughed and ruffled my hair and called me Little Miss Lucky.

When the typewriter came I got all in a muddle trying to open the box without taking the string off and Nanna said, *patience, patience,* and went to get the scissors. I wound in the special typewriting paper our Derek had brought from up the street and then I had to decide whether to flick onto the black or the red. I couldn't

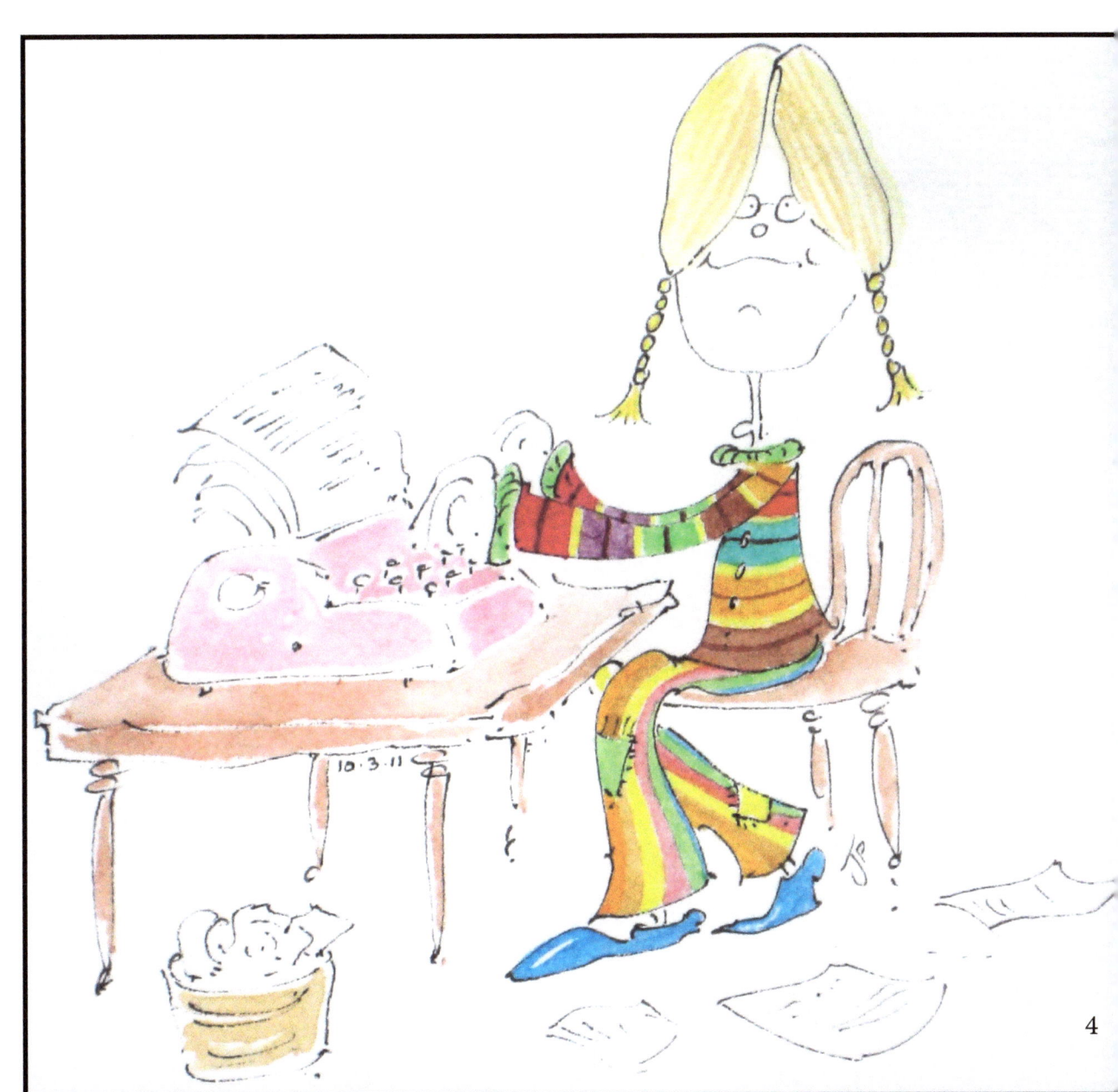

4

make my mind up so I had a go with both: I wrote 'the quick brown fox jumps over the lazy dog' in both colours and then in capitals and my grandfather said, *hey steady on lassie or your ribbon'll be needing changed before you've even started*, and I put my arms around his neck and said he was the best granda in the whole wide world even if he did have no teeth and smelt of remedies and he said not to talk so daft.

My typewriter had a special case that required some careful manoeuvring to get the lid back on and at first I got cross with it and tried to force it and Granda stood up and said, *no no no lassie, that's not the way to do it*. And he made me laugh even though I was cross because he said it in a funny gratey voice that sounded like Punch and Judy. He came to where I was kneeling on the carpet and he helped me get the lid on and that was the strangest thing because my grandfather never got up off his chair and he certainly wasn't supposed to walk across the floor. He had to get back double quick because we heard Nanna coming down the stairs with the hot water bottle and she looked worried when she saw him out of breath for no apparent reason.

That first day I typed up a poem about my dog that I had written specially. Granda said it was champion and I'd be writing books one day, and he slapped his leg as if he couldn't quite believe what he'd just said. I made a lovely pattern round the edge and coloured it in and wrote underneath in fancy writing to the bestest granda and Nanna said there was no such word. But she hung it up anyway, by a drawing pin, next to Granda's little water-colour of a mill in the Ouseburn Valley, remembered from when he was a lad, from before he got too sick through breathing in the industry that sunk down there, down around the cottages, down under the viaduct, from before all he'd grown up with had somehow fallen into rack and ruin.

Not long after, my grandfather died, peacefully in his sleep it was said, but I wondered how anyone would know that. *Oh, they know,* my nanna said, *they know alright.*

One day, a few weeks later, Mrs Robson came but Nanna was out cleaning. I was by myself and I asked politely *what can I do for you Mrs Robson.* She said, *Oh I've only just come for the typewriter money, but if your nanna's not here, well …* I asked how much it was. *A shilling, she said, for this month, and the same for last.* I gave her a two shilling piece out of the coal money and she said, *well that's all fettled then, a big weight off my mind.* When Nanna came in I didn't know what to say. I had to tell her something though because the coal man would come on Monday and she'd be short and there'd be ructions. My grandmother was cross and said whatever was I thinking of, and money didn't grow on trees. I said, *but I thought my granda won the pools*, and Nanna said, *well it just goes to show, doesn't it, you're not paid to think, and when I want you to think, I'll let you know.*

I was nine years old when I got that typewriter. I know it's strange to say, but it got much harder to write things after that. The words may have looked better, but they didn't sound the same, and sometimes they didn't feel like they were mine any more. Once they'd been clacked out key by key, they were changed, transformed by the machine, alien. I'd watch them scrolling up in front of me and I'd be filled with an unaccountable rage. At times I even fancied the machine was mocking me, appearing to be obedient while making secret mistakes. I would wrench the paper out in fury, making the machine jump.

And as for those packets of typewriting paper that our Derek was always bringing down from up the street, there evolved in my mind a horror of the blank page that, in the end, amounted to a physical revulsion.

On rainy days my grandmother would see me sitting around, at a loose end, or leaning on the kitchen doorpost, nothing to do. *The devil makes evil work for idle hands, she would say, go and find yourself something to do, for pity's sake.* I'd be halfway up the stairs when she'd shout, *Get your typewriter out, write a story.*

What they wanted had half become what I wanted and I did try to do it. But whatever it was that had been in me had secreted itself away. In its place, panic, loneliness, a desperate sense of obligation – to my grandfather, to my entire family, for the useless sacrifices they so willingly made. Their kind encouragement, nothing but a burden.

I still have my Lilliput, and I'm still afraid of that terrible tangle of love and anger and pity and shame and longing and guilt that I jammed in there the last time I forced the lid on.

About This Piece

'It piece began its life in an NCLA memoir course (Alison Light and Jackie Kay, 2010), prompted by the suggestion to focus on an object. The child's typewriter came to mind as an object in which were condensed themes and feelings that seemed important to explore. I like working in that dense borderland between fact and fiction, where memories take shape and the past emerges anew each time. This piece is part of my personal quest for belonging: in a family, in a class, in culture, in history.' Shelley Day Sclater.

About Shelley

She has been a lawyer and an academic psychologist and now writes fiction. She has completed the first draft of a novel and the first year of a p/t MA in Creative Writing at Newcastle University and has had several short stories published.

The Accidental Sufi Haiku

Polly Malone

The ivy that has grown over my foot and up around my ankle starts pulling, so I sit down. I am in the hall of the house, between the inner door and the door to the street. I don't know what it is called, this bit. If it was tacked on to the front of the house, it would be a porch, but it's not, so it isn't. It's where we put coats, boots, the barometer. I got this far and could go no further. I stood, with one hand closing the door behind me and the other ready to open the front door and then remembered I needed to set the alarm, in the hall, by the kitchen. My landlord is very particular about it. But I couldn't turn back. I am on my way to the sea, and I couldn't turn back.

For a while I stand still with my hand on the handle of the inner door. The warmth from my hand passes into the metal of the handle. The warmth from my heart, to my hand, to the door. Sunlight smatters in through the glass panel at the top of the front door and I can feel it hot on my head, from my hairline up. The letterbox is just below this panel, at eye level, unusual. My landlord says he had it moved, something about security. There is a faint smell of kelp.

In Jo's house this bit is called the decompression chamber. The mud stops here. She has an umbrella stand, as she is the kind of person who doesn't lose umbrellas. She has a row of pegs for coats and hats and scarves and shelves for boots and a cupboard for other things. The pegs and the shelves and the cupboard are painted blue. This is in Stroud, by the way. Here we have two brass coat hooks, the barometer and a small brown and white mat. On that are my boots, still wet. Under the mat is lino. Brown lino. And that's it.

When the temperature of my hand and the door handle achieves equilibrium, I feel safe to let go. I reach up for the knob to turn to release the lock to open the front door and repeat the process. This is good.

I think it was words that first slipped past me. I typed thing there first of all, instead of think. Elsewhere I wrote mine instead of mind. And one time it came out ming, which was fun. I wrote scientish instead of scientist. No wonder I didn't get that job. Here between the doors I can't help noticing that sometimes words are slippery, sometimes static. Sometimes words are traps. Sometimes words are the animals caught in the traps. Sometimes words are the howls of the animals caught in the traps. Blah blah blah. You get the idea. Remembering things needed more than remembering the names for things; hearing their names called, words ran away and hid. But it doesn't matter. I can still write a bowl of cherry stones if you need irony, a tree root cracking a pavement if you need progress. I can parse you a hissy fit should you require it, or be the scribe for a good old-fashioned sulk. The incredible sulk. I can rip and rend clothing just by thinking about it and when I actually write it, put it on paper, I become unstitched and naked. This is good.

I sing too, I sing with my mouth open. I sing hymns, nursery rhymes, football chants, but I never think to sing a lullaby and now I find this hard to believe. I sing rivers, I sing the moon. I sing tides and the telling of lies. I sing in old money, I sing metric, I sing refrains, exchanges, I sing the body electric. I sing what I know of the scriptures, I sing total bollocks. I can't sing. And then I start again at the beginning.

The sun is higher in the sky and less light comes in but it's not gloomy, not at all. I see all the shoes and boots lined up. Height order; my landlord sorts in height order, and I begin to think he's slightly mad. Wellies, two pairs, one green, one black, then baseball boots, ankle boots with heels – probably his girlfriend's – fucking ugly crocs, trainers times four, work shoes, mules, slippers and slipper socks, all balled up and flung in a corner. Rebels. Where have my boots gone, all wet from the beach? I can't find them although I search thoroughly. I become convinced the tide has taken them. I am tidal. I am a windfall apple. The ivy pulls me and I sit down. This mat is futile. A weave of something man-made, made by a machine. Opposite me and up a bit are the coats, these are sorted by colour. A black leather jacket, a dark grey great coat, a blue anorak, a duffle-coat-coloured duffle coat, an off-white straight jacket and pure white wings, angel wings.

On the Metro I become convinced I could make a perfectly good living making and selling pinstripe hats. This is not such a bad idea. I draw out the design in the mud from my boots. On the Metro I take it personally when they say 'Doors Closing'. Going up the escalator I notice that the handrail goes faster than the stairs. I watch as my hand moves away from me, feeling my arm stretched gently. I climb up a step to catch up with myself.

The day's post falls down on my head. I call out 'thank you'. I tuck the letters safe in my boots. I don't go out much. I sit with my neighbours in their kitchen, smoking and laughing. I don't smoke.

At the beach, I walk up to the promontory. I sit on the bench with the plaque that says: 1948 – 2004 Mrs Chand Jairath – Always in our heart. To the left is Miss Sarita Jairath 1973 – 2005. You are always with us. She must be Mrs Jairath's daughter. I can never decide if it is good her mother didn't live to see her die, or not. And to the right, past the bin, are Rhoda and Bobby Dyer – Sunny Memories. They loved this view. There's nothing to see but the sea and the sky. That's it. I think: that's all you need. I want my plaque on the bin between them. Then I can be filled with … the things other people no longer need, I want. I can be filled and emptied, filled and emptied forever.

I become the Netherlands. Flat earth held up by my own compacted past. My own personal landfill. I become convinced that time, especially the past and the future, has a force as strong as gravity or magnetism. It pulls us backwards and pushes us forwards. It is this that makes us hungry, this that gives us the certainty of death, of reaching the full stop. I think I think that the reason we don't time travel is that we never stay still long enough for time to get a beam on us. Until we're dead. So we fear death because we don't know where it will take us. We'll be snatched up by time and thrown about, temporally. Eternity, we talk about that. But we don't get it.

I am hungry. I heard somewhere that ravelled and unravelled mean the same thing and I'd go and check this on the Internet but I need to stay here, between the doors, waiting for time. My coat pockets are weighed down with the pieces of worn glass I pick up from the beach. Sand, glass, sand.

A spider has spun a web over my foot, like something out of Lilliput. I believe gravity is personal and will decide to keep me here, tethered on the ground, safe from spinning off, if only I am good enough. I watch the spider make more webs. I watch the birds build nests, I watch a city rise, thrive and fall within seven days and nights.

I call in well to work and they say don't you mean ill and I try to explain and then halfway through I realise I have put the phone down like you would a half dead cat. It is a mercy killing.

I go to lectures I go to workshops I go to the pub to meet Ira. I am bombarded by synchronicity, by serendipity. He says it is serendipity do dah. There's some hoo hah about memoir. Before I can form the question, I'm told the answer. I take to the streets, I take to the beach. I take to getting up when it's dark to watch the sun rise. I stay there all day so I can see it again. I stay where I am.

My hands are crossed over my shoulders. My palms flat against the wall on either side of my head. It was hard to take my hands from the doors but now I've done it, I rejoice. I think of geckos and how now they think that the pads on their feet are not sticky. No. They form a light covalent bond with the wall, animal and mineral. In Zanzibar the geckos came to my room when I invited them in. There was a mesh over the window but they still came in. I called to the bush babies and they came too, but remained at a polite distance, outside, in the trees. Here the best I can muster is a spider. In the Spring I will try for moths.

It is dark. My lover comes. We take the glass pebbles from my pockets and spread them under us. White, blue, green. We tell each other stories. I tell him about my special powers. When I go to poetry readings, the poets always read my favourite pieces. You can check this. Recent examples? Carol Ann Duffy read Syntax and I nearly fainted. Seamus Heaney read the one about St Kevin and the Blackbird. Sharon Olds (this was in a big cold church in Bath, by the way) read the one about seeing her bum in a full-length mirror. Desmond Graham (who doesn't believe in punctuation) read the one about a comma being a random squashed insect. I am beginning to believe it works for prose too – Sean O'Brien read the trippy party part of his novel. I wanted him to and he did. I knew he would. But then again, he is a poet, so that doesn't prove anything. My lover tells me the story behind the song. He tells me he is as constant as the northern star and if I need him he'll be in the bar. I say he's cheating, that's Joni, if memory serves me. I say I am constantly in the dark and if he needs me I'll be in the park. I'm lying though and he knows it. The estuary pulls me. Silt builds up between us. I tell him grief is silt and he knows it's true. We name the seven dwarves, the seven deadly sins, the seven muses, the seven cities of the apocalypse. We agree that nothing clinical can ever be beautiful, that truth is a mess and religion an excuse.

Then I am his bed and he is mine. Our close kiss press, our body meld and mesh, our skin, our beginnings and endings, carry us through the night. We leave no moan unheard. Try as we might, we can't resist the buoyancy of morning. Will you stay here? he asks me.

Tomorrow I go back to the beach. On the way I will go to the bakery. There are two loaves that look so beautiful I can't decide between them. The lady in the shop says; Make your mind up. Come on, love, I haven't got all day. Make up your mind.

I think: I will. This is good work to do at the seaside. I either need a tether for my boat, or a string for my

9

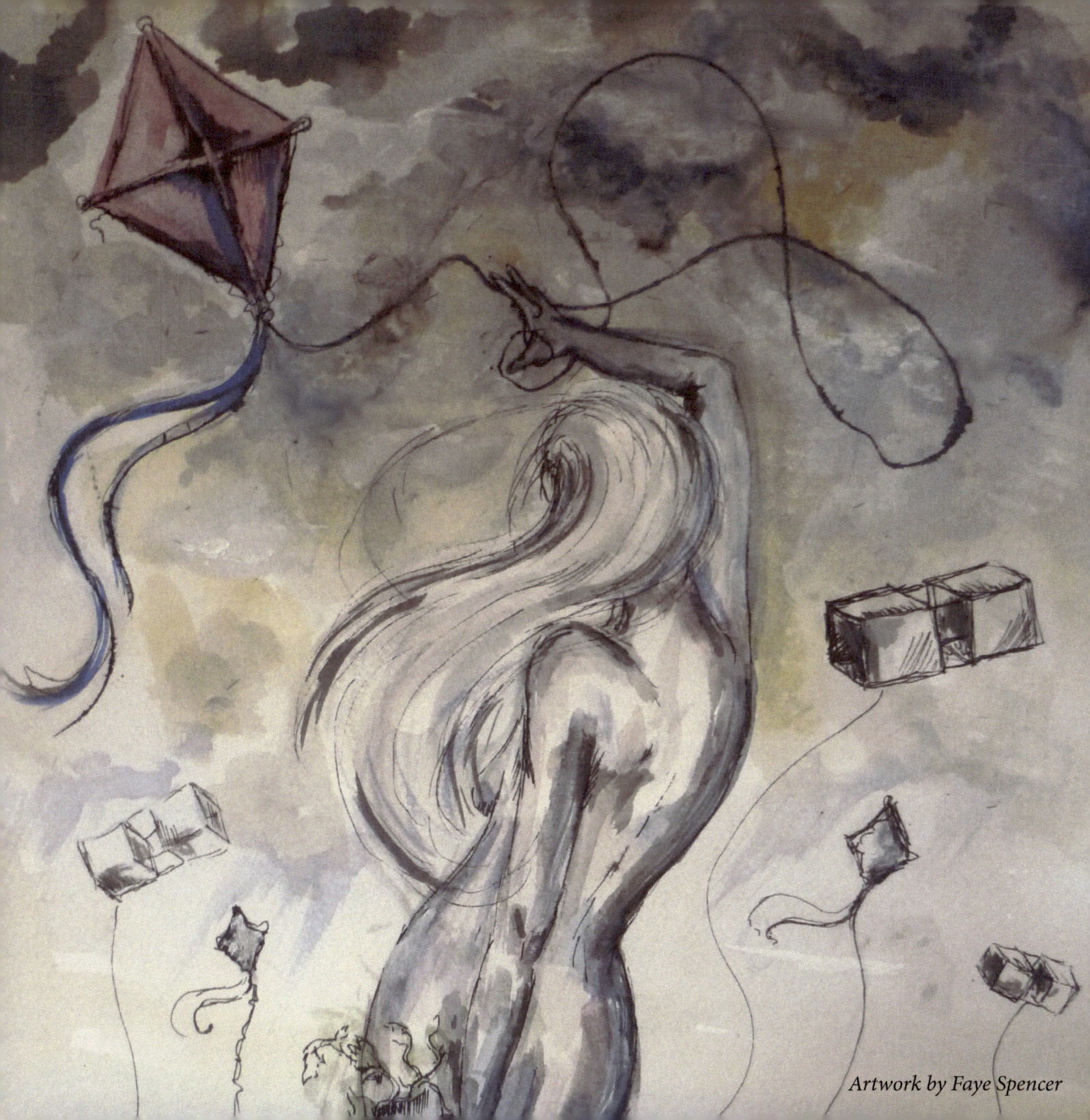

Artwork by Faye Spencer

kite. Unravel, ravel. Either/both. Some tactile connection between heaven and earth. I make it from the parts of my sisters I miss; sturdy love and a happy knack with leftovers. I throw in camaraderie and bravery from my imaginary brother. I weave in the part of Welcome that isn't the mat, the purr from a happy cat, the shadow that contains the bat. I put in the bit of the net that isn't the thread, the point of no return, the thought that counts. I put in empty. I put in plenty. And Mind The Gap since I've taken that to stitch in alongside deep space and that Atlantis place. I put in the in-breath before the words begin when Julian sings and the pause before the applause when his song is sung. I put in the beat of love that's given freely. I put in the heart of the night, the heat of the moment.

I test its tensile strength. There will be repairs necessary. There will be times the kite will crash to the ground/be lost in the clouds or the boat will disappear over the horizon/be lost in the clouds. There will be perfect flying days and a good catch. I take out my notebook and I write

I write kite strings
Reaching up
Striving to link
Heaven and earth with ink
I don't have a pen.

I see a priest and go to him and together we praise the pioneers, the pyromaniacs and the prison warders. We bless the meddlers, the peddlers and the administrators. I give thanks for the spider that kept me on the ground all that time. I don't think about the ivy.

With the last of my strength I go to the city. I go to the bookshops and shake all the words out of all the books. I pay special attention to the self-help section. I buy all the pens and hand them out, one by one, to everyone at the counter. I give them with love. This is good.

I stand at the edge of the sea again. I don't go in. What, do you think I'm mad? It would be certain death with all these glass songs in my pockets. What, do you think I should? You're probably right. I name the seven waves for the seven stories. On the way home I look at the two loaves again. I buy sunflowers. The kite is an illustrated, illuminated manuscript. The boat is a coracle.

Once inside, once upon a time, I sit down and, slipshod, I shed the sea. If you need me again look for me under your boot-soles.

About The Piece

'It was inspired by the Creative Writing and Psychology course in Newcastle University – and by the benches along the sea front in Whitley Bay. I wanted to explore a mental breakdown – and a mental re-build.'

About Polly

She was born in a corridor and now lives next to a graveyard. She's had a few proper jobs but is no good at being told what to do. She writes because is something she can do – without having to iron any clothes. She's a cracking good editor (highly recommended by this mag's editor herself), should anyone need one…

The Final Departure

Catherine Mccallum

Afterwards Charles could not have told you why he looked up when he did. He had been engrossed by news of the revised national budget by Peterborough and by the time the train pulled into York he was flicking past what seemed like the third appeal that week for anything he could spare for the victims of the latest flood, earthquake or famine. But for some reason he did glance up. Perhaps it was the sudden coughing from the opposite end of the carriage that stirred him. Perhaps if someone had not been so eager to tip their last few salted peanuts to the back of their throat there would now be no disturbance for the rest of the carriage to silently resent and, just perhaps, he wouldn't have seen her.

She was sitting on the floor at the end of the vestibule, her back resting lightly against the glass partition and her knees pulled high to her chest, as though she was anticipating a large influx of others to squeeze in and join her in her apparent rejection of the various empty seats dotted throughout the train. As it was, however, she found herself left alone to peer out beyond the tracks into the dim early morning light over the distant rooftops, where still some street lamps strained to cling to their nightly sovereignty. She did not seem troubled exactly— no, that would have been too easy to assume—she was more distant, as though had you seen her anywhere, you would have observed the same vacant expression and the same detachment from her surroundings. There seemed to be a certain fragility about her—that was unarguable—but whether this came from her being alone, her nervous chipping away at her nail polish or the way her cardigan draped over her slender frame he was not sure. But as she carelessly moved her hands up to lift the body of chestnut hair that came falling around her face and guide it to rest over her left shoulder, Charles was struck by her beauty—simple and subtle as it was. It was the beauty that endures with youth and, while he fought every impulse dragging him back, he could not help but see the similarity. He longed desperately to stay there, amongst the coughing and the sports pages, where he could forget and ignore. But he had seen into her eyes, with the same distant and hopeful gaze that he had seen in someone else so long ago.

They too had been young, of course, as it is with many a person's story bearing that particular kind of significance and truth: those stories that seem to sustain such a hold on us, embedding themselves so deep into our memories that we hardly know where we'd be, or who we'd be without them. Yet how abruptly they can be exhumed; how easily the vaguest resemblance or the weakest stimuli can undermine the work of years, where the sting of past pain had so steadily become soothed.

Charles had never even intended to meet anyone like her; his heart had been far too consumed by hopes revolving around his writing. He would make his way to London once he had graduated—the only place for any aspiring writer, he had heard—live in a single bedroom apartment near the West End, buying theatre tickets instead of groceries and sipping coffee instreet corner cafés. He did get there eventually, of course, but it was not in the manner in which he had intended; there was so much more, too many interruptions, yet to come.

It was barely the autumn of 1937 when he first made his way up from Manchester Piccadilly to university. He could still recall the advice that people had so often spewed forth when he spoke of his plans back home, and how often he had ignored them. The neighbours' doubt and derisions had lain dormant in his mind—he was a working man's lad and mustn't forget it, after all—and yet he knew that with every mile the tracks led him further and further away from all of that. Every slight shudder of the wheels connecting with the track reverberated through his fingertips arched upon the armrest, right through to his very being, right to his core. The anticipation was almost tangible. He had never been quite as romantic as people had supposed, however, and had realised that Oxbridge was indeed out of the question, of course; even the most liberally minded Oxford don would hardly see him sporting his father's best corduroy Sunday suit, hear the accent and spring to welcome him with open arms and an open pocket to the college scholarship fund. No, he had decided upon Durham, where he wouldn't need to show his face until it was too late for them to change their minds.

Alighting now from the train nearly sixty years on, it all seemed so long ago that he had begun his journey bursting into the station and his new life, his new chance. How different he had felt. Slowly, carefully, he now relieved himself of his small leather satchel and brought himself upright upon his stick so as to be able to survey the station that he knew so well. Everything seemed unchanged—the distant cathedral, the chipped woodwork of the benches; even today's train controller wore the same exasperated expression characteristic of the profession—and through the fog behind his glasses he could almost see her, waving him into the station, books in hand for the term ahead. He knew that in allowing himself even that meagre glimpse into his past he had made a mistake; it came upon him inevitably within mere moments without any possibility of anaesthetising censoring. He was rushed onwards two years later to that fateful November morning: the very last time he saw her. She had been standing upon the edge of the very platform where he now found himself lingering, with the smoke of the departing train billowing round her, merciless and suffocating. Her woollen shawls enveloped her, clung to her, clung to all they had been, all they should have been and all that they no longer could be. He had tried so desperately not to look back, to keep his thoughts on duty and not to allow himself to see her distant frame slowly and torturously drift away from sight, growing fainter and fainter as he drew further away from that place, where every part of himself and his future were left behind with her.

They had always known that that day would come, however, ever since they had crowded around the wireless amongst their fellow students and heard the announcement that we were, indeed, at war with Germany. Others had been excited, others indifferent, but it was at that moment they saw that their time together had been made finite. King and country would soon come knocking; Charles had no choice but to be ready to answer.

And yet the night before he left there would be no acknowledgement of their impending separation, no frantic embrace of those last hours. The pair of them told themselves that endings were for others to endure and yet the air was heavy with an unspoken, impenetrable resignation. They lay rigid on their backs, eyes fixed upon the ceiling, hardly uttering a word, almost touching, barely breathing. Never once did they betray their gaze to the nightstand at the left side of the bed, upon which lay Charles' conscription papers.

He became aware that at some point during the course of his mesmerism, his hand had eased its way deep into his jacket pocket, to the small slip of paper that it had found there. He paused there for a moment, tracing his fingers along its folds and creases, before peering down to the words that he need not even read; he knew the article's content all too well. It had been a stray bomb—unintended, inconsequential—and yet the list before him stood as proof of its magnitude. Third from the bottom, an inch above a slight tear in the page from back in the sixties, was her name.

He replaced the relic and began to make his way through the city towards the cathedral. They had told him that his heart may not hold out much longer and that he may not even see the new year, but that was of no real concern to him. He was back where he started and now, finally, he was done. His long battle with time, its constraints and its pressures had left him forlorn, empty and utterly alone. He had survived, yes, but as he stood at his pew amongst the deafening silence on the last Remembrance Day the doctors could promise him, he couldn't help but think that he had barely survived survival.

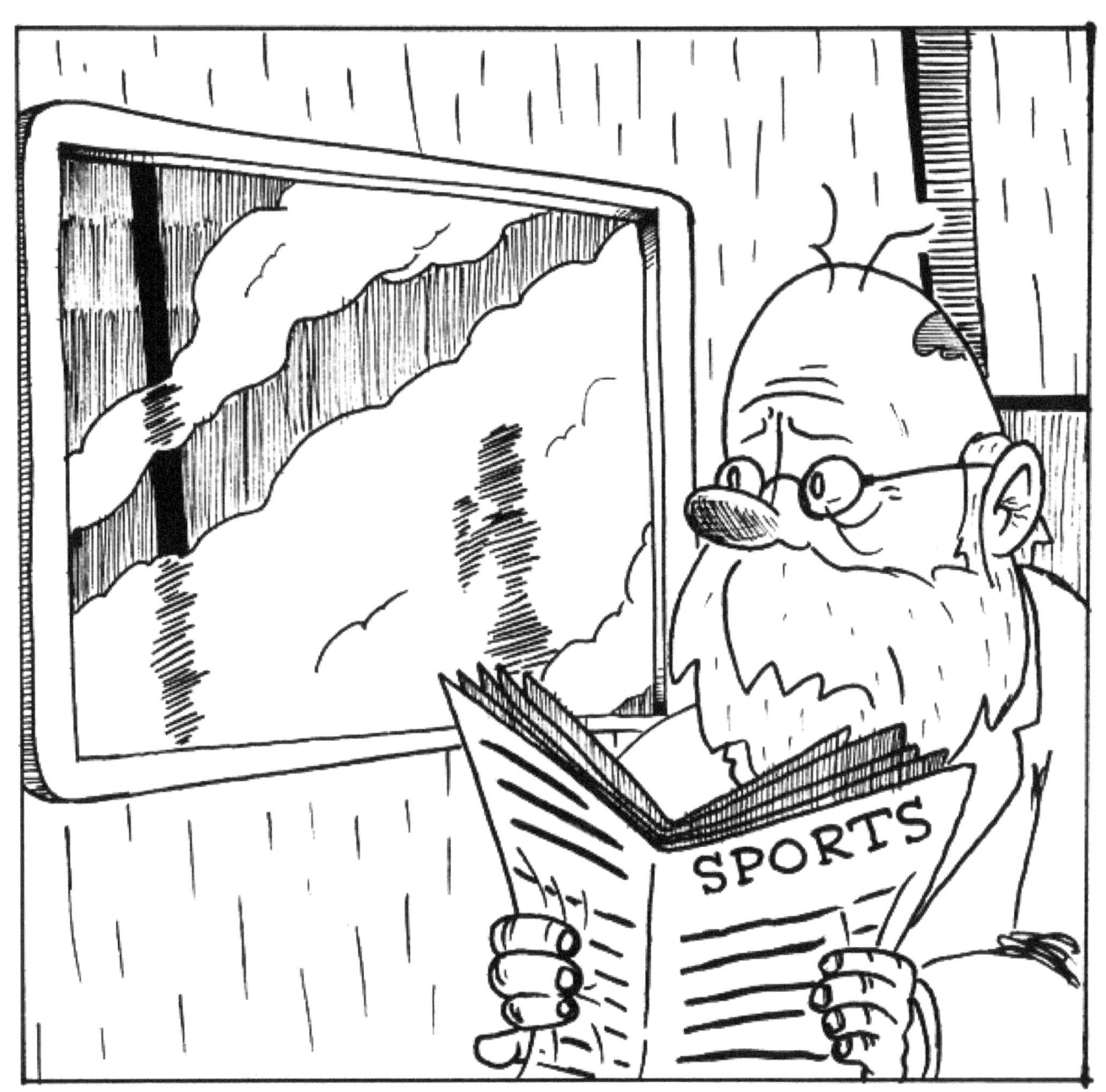

Artwork by Jonathan David Lim.

The Lake

Emily Nicholson

Headed for the lake he carried the child bundled in cloth. The ground slopped as he trod the earth. With each stride the cloth slipped a little and his huge hands pulled up the bundle in awkward jerks.

He had reached the wood and could hear the wails of the mother from the cottage. Cut loose from the mother's cord. Out of the watery womb. The child slipped again and he tugged it with his hands. He felt the baby fluid, milk congealed with tears and fresh skin against the rough wrinkles of his fingers. The child started to howl.

The sound of screams grew silent and the child grew silent and cold. The woods swallowed sound except for the birds that cawed. He trudged on. He beat back the brambles and trampled over roots and leaves.

The path grew dense and it was all forest and trees and overgrowth. Pushing back a vine it swung back in an arch swipe. It caught his cheek and scratched the child's forehead. It caught his dry skin and blood began to trickle. He brushed his cheek with the back of his hand.

The child let out a wail. The skin was scarred and it was marked red. The child eyed the man. He looked at the child. It was wriggling. Its eyes darted from side to side. He reached out his forefinger and moved it to the child. The child beat its arms and arced its back in protest. Gently he brushed the scar with his finger.

Ahead the air was lighter. It was the reflection of the lake. He walked towards the water. At the shoreline he stood in his large soiled boots. In his hands he gripped the child.

The sun was beginning to rise and it turned the skyline to embers. He did not look for his reflection. He walked into the water. Up to his boots in lake he looked down. The child wrinkled its blotched skin and its eyes shone wet in the dawn light. It writhed in his hands under its cloth but he held tighter. Thinking of the new day he opened his arms.

About Emily
She was born in 1988 in Huntingdon. The Lake was inspired by a painting by Peter Doig. It is her first published story. She currently lives in Newcastle.

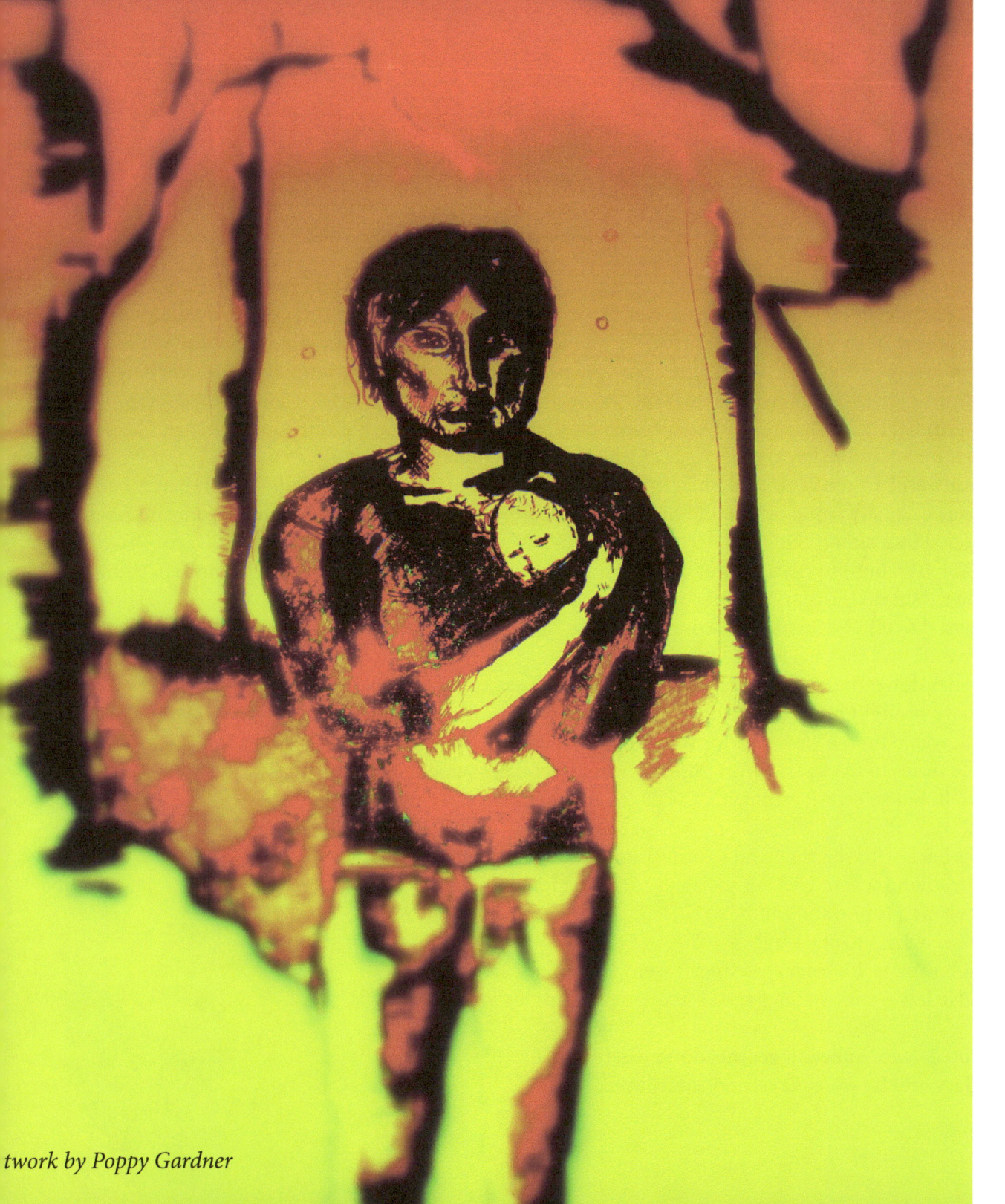

twork by Poppy Gardner

18

Low Tide

Patrick Robertson

On a bench overlooking the slow curve of the seafront sits a small man in glasses and brown slacks. By now, he blends into the landscape, his eyes having faded over the years until their grey-blue tint exactly matches the sea. The light changes all the time, from sunny morning to cloudy afternoon to overcast twilight, but the sea seems to be the same colour always. It's early evening now. Tiny people buried in coats are scattered about, creeping home. The man takes off his glasses and polishes them with a steadiness of motion that betrays a long-held habit.

He is interrupted by another man, whose frame is taller, his hair longer, his shirt open further. Get this down you, he says, his voice louder, and hands him a beer from the pub behind.

Simon James and Simon McDonald had known each other too long to stay friends. Simon James had a thousand nicknames, usually Jamie or Jim, but Simon McDonald had never been more than Simon, and finally the name had eroded into simply "Si".

Sit down, Si says, but Jim doesn't often sit down. He paces and fidgets like a child, and thinks Si sounds more like his father than his partner. "Partner" wasn't even a word Jim would ever have used before he met Si. He would have said "lover", but Si always said "husband", and they eventually met in the middle.

Jim crunches down the seashell beach to the brink of the ocean. Today the tides have brought him a bright bivalve shell, richly orange in the half-light. Si stays up on the concrete. He is a writer of romances, with a mildly profitable series to his name. With him as always is a pad of paper. He sets the pen to it, but the wind is blowing the pages about and he can't get a word down.

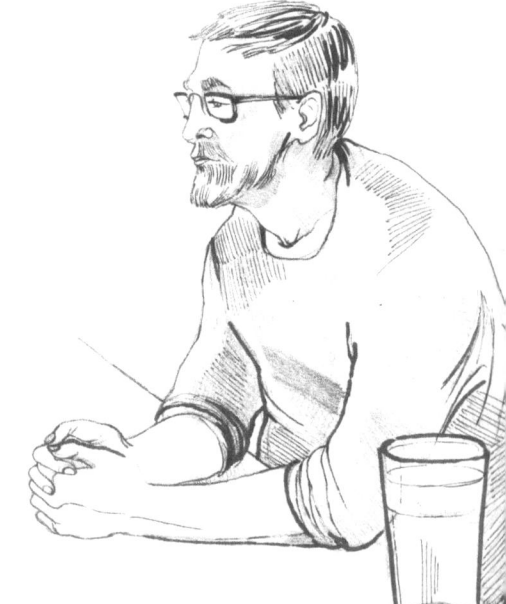

Jim comes back with the shell and says, let's go into town tonight. He waves at the headland where you can see a corner of the town poking out, up where the beach is fine and sandy.

Why, says Si, what's happening?

Anything, Jim says. It's been ages since I went. This is not strictly true. It's Sunday. He last went two days ago. The town is where his job is, in a patent office.

Si says, you can go. I need to get this done. There'll be nothing happening. Sundays are the worst days, and Saturdays.

Monday. On the local news, someone had gone out to the shore on a foggy evening and got surrounded by the tide. Poor guy had drowned. They show an interview with the wife in her grey living room, her face craggy and worn away. It makes Si nervous. He often wandered the beach in the evening, enjoying the peace and quiet.

Jim comes home a few minutes later than usual, and Si meets him in the hallway and holds him tight. Jim still has the cold air caught in his hair and the folds of his clothes. He is confused, but he hugs Si back.

That night, a gust of wind reaches in through the window and Si nuzzles into Jim fiercely. Half-asleep, Jim feels in the embrace something warm and intense that he has not felt in months. They throw off the covers and make love, naked and open, and fall asleep against the cold night.

The morning is equally cold, and Si finds himself alone; Jim has left for work. Usually he inadvertently wakes Si as he gets out of bed, but Si is becoming a heavier sleeper.

Si tries to work too. He goes round the seafront with his notebook and sits in a dozen places. The cheap plastic tables at the cafe. The teashop with wrought-iron furniture set out under thick umbrellas. The plush pub seats. Nowhere gives him a story. Eventually he settles on some steps, tucked away under the pier. The tide is out, the beach is empty.

Enough of this nonsense, Si thinks. Writer's block is such a juvenile thing. It sounds grand but all it really is is laziness, and at his age Si should be well over it. So he does what he always does when he can't think of anything better – he looks back over his old characters, plucks out a couple at random and sets them against each other. They can't be the same as before, of course. Tweak the dials a bit. An intelligence upgrade, a sense of humour bypass, and they're good as new.

And that goes a little better. Daisy and Stephen meet each other on a train, and she is charmed by his wit, and he admires her long chestnut hair – chestnut is a good colour for hair – and they continue in this vein for about three thousand words. A good day's work, all in all, considering the slow start. Si packs up.

Jim dawdles on the way home and gets in late again. Si greets him warmly, dinner comes out of the oven and they watch television. No bad news tonight. Everything is fine. Jim remembers to close the bedroom window and Si slips off to sleep almost immediately

Si wakes in the night. Lying there in the dark, he becomes aware that Jim is also awake.

Hey, what's up? Si says, uncomfortable, like he has stumbled into something private.

Nothing's up.

Why are you awake?

I'm just awake. Jim sounds irritated.

All right, says Si, and rolls over.

After a moment, Jim says, I can't sleep for some reason.

Si wriggles into a half-sitting position. Have a hot drink, or read a book.

Tried that already.

Well, I don't know what to suggest. Si says. Jim doesn't move. His eyes are closed.

Anything I can do?

Jim shrugs, rustling the bedclothes.

Si shuffles back down into the covers and tries to sleep again. It takes a little longer this time. He feels uneasy, as if he is leaving Jim behind.

Morning. Si wakes late again, cold again, missing Jim again. He looks back at what he's written. In the watery morning sunlight the words are flat and empty. He will have to frustrate the romance somehow. In the hour that follows, he marries both his protagonists to offstage spouses, blinds Stephen, makes Daisy a kleptomaniac, and eventually derails their train into a heavily populated area, maiming them both beyond all hope of recovery. It results in a good three pages of clutter and crossings-out, and Si takes great pleasure in tearing them out and feeding them into the shredder. It is going to be one of those days.

So he abandons his notebook for lunch, and turns on the computer. A pleasant surprise: in among the junk emails is one from a fan, a Mrs. Anne Turlough. Si is unaccustomed to fan letters, but has received enough to know that between the outbreaks of praise they tend to always say the same things, and this one does nothing to break the trend. *Have you always wanted to be an author? How do you get into writing?* Even: *Where do you get your ideas?*

Si puts fingers to the keyboard for a reply. *No, I wanted to be a chimney sweep, but I'm not tall enough.* Delete; *Yes, I always wanted to be a writer.* As if there was any other answer. *To get into writing one requires a strong work ethic, knowledge of one's audience, and large reserves of discipline. Where do I get my ideas?* Why do they always ask that? Si leans back and looks out of the window at the little waves steadily folding themselves up the beach. With a smile, he types: *The tides bring them.*

After sending his reply, he pastes the email into Word and saves it: one of his few indulgences. Except his mouse slips on the menu and he opens up something else by accident. Something from the "Recent Documents" list.

It's a file Si hasn't seen before. *A Hundred Things to Do Before You Die,* it says, and a list. *Go to Egypt. Learn to play the guitar. Get a tattoo.* Si scrolls down. There aren't a hundred things there, it must be a work in progress, but there are quite a few.

Si hits Print in a sort of daze. The printer obligingly churns out the pages, three of them. Staring at them, Si imagines for a crazy moment that he'd written the list himself and forgotten about it. Although he's fairly sure he's never wanted a pool table, or to go to Amsterdam.

An hour after the usual time, Jim's key turns in the lock. When he comes into the living room Si does not even greet him, just holds the list out. Jim reads, and then looks up at Si's expectant expression, and after a moment just says, yeah?

Si asks, when did you… when did you write this?

Jim shrugs.

How many did you end up doing?

Some of them.

How many?

Jim half-snaps, what do you mean, end up?

Si doesn't say anything.

I haven't ended up. And he switches the television on and won't say another word.

Si withdraws from the room and feeds the list into the shredder, where it joins Stephen and Daisy in a tangled heap in the waste-paper basket. He decides to take an early night, and is asleep before Jim comes up to join him.

Thursday crawls emptily by. Si knows that this is the time of life when men start having mid-life crises, but the thought had never given him much concern before. He had had a mid-life crisis at the age of nineteen, and then another, smaller one at twenty-four, and since then things had been more or less steady. As for Jim, Si hadn't expected him to have one at all. He didn't think he'd get that far.

In between these sorts of thoughts Si tries to think of Stephen and Daisy, but they prove reluctant to be resurrected. Daisy is a thoroughly uninspiring character, and Stephen is stubbornly refusing to get involved in any plot Si can think of.

He writes them off as a bad job, and resolves to begin anew. But it's easier said than done. Any ideas he can muster die as soon as they have appeared, and paranoia and anxiety bubble up around them. Si cannot distract himself with anything. It is a frustrating day.

Jim is early home.

Let's go into town tonight, Si says. I'm bouncing off the bloody walls. And you have the day off tomorrow. Come on.

Jim seems oddly reluctant, but Si won't take no for an answer. He has cooked dinner already. Si is lively and talkative as they eat; Jim is distant and withdrawn.

They catch the bus. Jim takes the window seat and stares. Buildings grow higher as they slide by, like the sides of a canyon descending into the ground. Si starts to feel nervous for reasons he cannot explain. The journey has the opposite effect on Jim: he grows visibly more comfortable as they draw into town, and is the first to get up when the bus stops.

A wave of noise hits as the doors open. They disembark under a flickering streetlight. Si puts a hand on the pole as if the stream of people on the street will carry him away. Where to? he is about to ask, but Jim has already spotted someone he knows, and plunges into the crowd. Uncertainly, Si follows.

Jim is in his element. He whirls from bar to bar, every inch the social butterfly. Barely a moment goes by without him raising a glass to someone, or receiving a pat on the back, or a kiss on the cheek. He shouts, and laughs, and says more in an hour than he has said to Si in weeks.

To Si it is all just a wall of light. He gets tired of hanging on Jim's sleeve and asking who was that with every greeting, and instead focuses on the alcohol as if it will make sense of things. All it does is steadily reduce his ability to block out the background noise. The relentless babble, nebulous and menacing, rises to smother him. Lamps tilt, swim and gain halos.

In a club where the lights flash a relentless rainbow disco, Si shelters in a toilet cubicle. It's a slight respite even though the smell of detergent makes him nauseous. Someone is having sex in the next-door cubicle, and the man on the other side babbles into a phone as he pisses. Si has had enough.

Leaving the toilet, he pushes his way through to Jim, who is half-dancing with a couple of men Si doesn't recognise. He tugs on Jim's sleeve and shouts into his ear, let's go.

Jim can't hear. Let's go, Si tries again.

Let's have one more, Jim shouts back. You'll feel better.

Can we go, please? Si feels like a child, repeating himself, bellowing at Jim through the noise. The effort pushes out a few frustrated tears.

Jim looks at him and just says: you can go. And the look on his face, almost scornful, is quite unlike him. Like Si is a stranger.

It is as if the look pushes them apart. Si stares. The two men have never been very alike, but in this moment Si cannot see anything of himself in Jim. There is not an atom of him left. The night has washed Jim clean. Si barely recognises what's underneath.

The road leads straight back home, but Si needs to get away from people. It is slightly quicker to walk along the coast. The beach ought to be empty on a cold night like this.

It is indeed empty, and cold: colder than Si had realised. The warmth of the town does not extend very far down the hill. As he moves away from the orange-lit streets, down the steep steps to the black, moonless beach, he meets a wall of chilly air, like darkness gone solid. His feet touch sand. He'd expected to find a path, but it does not start until further along the coast. He starts to walk, regardless. The danger does not even occur to him.

The sea has taken on the colour of night. It lies on the beach like oil, gleaming, waiting. And then the town disappears around the bend and it loses its gleam. The moon, unseen, is pulling. The sea extends an inky finger silently across the sand.

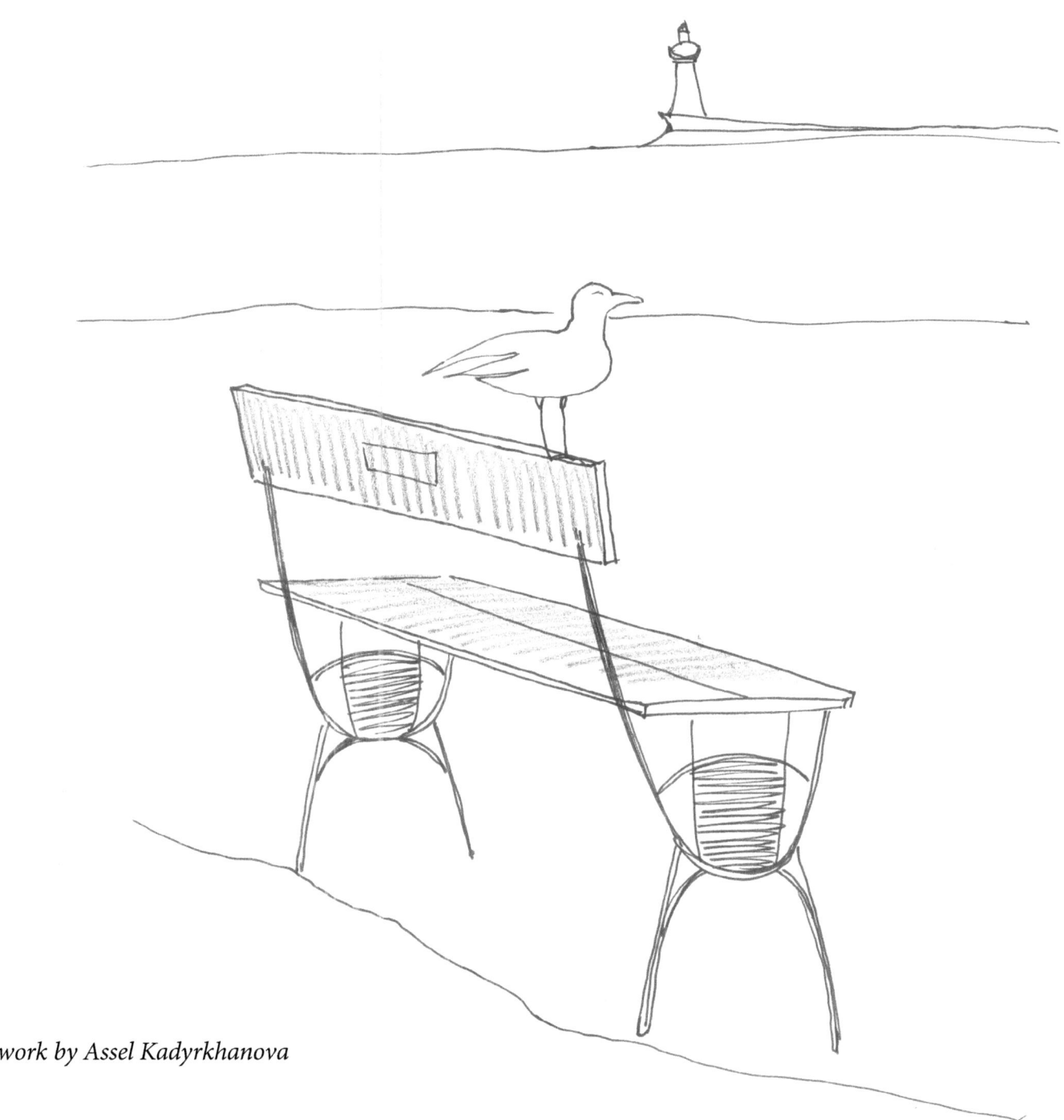

Artwork by Assel Kadyrkhanova

Shallow, it brushes Si's shoes so gently that he does not even notice. He is walking briskly, concentrating on going in the right direction. Afraid of walking into the cliff in the dark, he is slowly veering away from the land.

The wind strikes up as he comes further away from the cliff. Another black finger of water glides up the shore. The sea is quietly swelling, gathering around Si, drawing him in. Still unnoticed, it pushes another shallow layer under his feet. There is a soft spitter-spatter as he walks, but the sound is swallowed by the wind. The layer fattens, creeping higher.

There is a change of texture underfoot, the sand giving way to tiny shards of shell and grit. Si's footsteps begin to crunch, and this is what makes him finally look down and see the water thickening around him, crawling up his shoes and dampening the edges of his trousers.

Smothering a jolt of fear, he quickens his pace, and tries to judge his distance from home by the coarseness of the beach. It is still fine, sinking away under his feet, each shallow footprint lingering for a second before being swallowed up by the encroaching sea. It seems impossible to him that he has wandered into danger so unthinkingly, no matter how disorientated the night has left him. The wind is wailing unrestrainedly. Abandoning his pride, Si runs.

The beach deepens. Si finds the water halfway to his knees and thrashes through, fearful that every step might take him further down. His lungs gasp fitfully as if the water is filling them.

And suddenly he is belted in the stomach, the wind is knocked out of him, and he almost falls. He clutches at the thing he has run into, and his fingers feel rotten, water-fattened wood – a groyne. He clings to it gratefully, even before his knowledge of the beach kicks in and he remembers that the groynes signal the start of the path. He fumbles along the structure, feeling the water relinquish its grip as he moves higher, and eventually finds the metal railing. He pulls himself up onto the path and squats there, gritty and waterlogged and exhausted.

He knows the path leads home, but he does not feel truly safe until he has trudged the full distance to his house and stands dripping on the carpet.

Si finds the bedclothes undisturbed in the morning. Jim is a restless sleeper: it is clear he has not returned.

Si gets up and eats breakfast in a sort of automatic way. He gets out his phone to send Jim a text message, but can't think of what to say. In the end he just asks where he is. There is no immediate reply.

Outside the window the beach lies there, grey and tranquil, showing no sign of its nocturnal menace. After breakfast Si goes out with his notebook and sits on a bench close to the house. The seafront is deserted, devoid of both people and ideas. Si cannot write a thing.

By lunchtime he knows Jim is not coming back.

Maybe he will return to pick up his belongings, and offer some sort of explanation, but he won't stay. The sea has lost its grip on him. He is not the same person who used to live here.

Si wonders if he could get away too. Get a house in town, or move further inland, maybe go back to his parents in the city, get a new job, meet new people… the thought makes him dizzy. What is keeping him here? But the same time, what is out there for him?

Si turns over his pad and writes on the last page, A Hundred Things To Do Before You Die, and he writes a little "1", neatly, and marks it with a dot. And then he just sits there because he can't think of anything to put down. Not a thing. Not a single solitary thing.

Ahead, the waves slip over each other, tugging at the beach, pulling grains of shell and sand down the shore and into the sea where they sink, settle, and rest forever.

About The Piece
'The story is set on a particular beach in Wales: not so much the physical details, I've changed most of those, but the feeling I got from it, of what kind of person would live there, at what stage in their life, and what might happen to them. It's also partly a comment on the kind of writer I really don't want to be.'

About Patrick
He's a Creative Writing student originally from London.

On Hope
Sherezade García Rangel

EARLY EVENING. OLD COUPLE, MAN AND WOMAN, STANDING AT THE PROMENADE OF THE TYNE, DRINKING AND EATING. SOUNDS OF RIVER.

MAN: It's been years.

WOMAN: Yes.

MAN: Hasn't changed that much now.

WOMAN: It's changed some.

MAN: Some, (BEAT) you can say it's changed some.

WOMAN: I don't remember how it was.

MAN: That's because you are too old to remember.

WOMAN: I'm younger than you.

MAN: That doesn't make you young.

WOMAN: Not young, but younger.

MAN: What's younger gonna do for you?

WOMAN: It'll do enough. I'll be the last to get a hip replacement!

MAN: The last of whom?

WOMAN: The last of you.

MAN: (PAUSE) Here's me thinking, what are you going to do with a new hip?

WOMAN: Same I did with my last one.

MAN: Wear it out?

WOMAN: Use it wisely.

MAN: I'll have some people to testify you did nothing of the sort with the original one.

WOMAN: You never complained.

MAN: I guess not. No good reason to. Your old hip's just fine.

WOMAN: (PAUSE) Nothing old is just fine anymore. It's just old.

MAN: What's wrong with old?

WOMAN: I'm wrong with old. Took me all that long just to get back here.

MAN: What's the rush?

WOMAN: No rush, I just want to know I can do it faster.

MAN: I thought you didn't like faster.

WOMAN: Walk faster.

MAN: Oh.

WOMAN: I just feel too old.

MAN: (BEAT) you are not too old, you are just…

WOMAN: Old?

MAN: Old enough.

WOMAN: Funny, that only sounds good when you are young.

MAN: (BEAT) Alright, think of it this way. You are old enough to be back here now, drinking what you are drinking, at this hour, in my presence.

WOMAN: I was never old enough for your presence.

MAN: Are you suggesting I did something…immoral?

WOMAN: Immoral? Illegal.

MAN: You were old enough back then too. I checked, your father checked.

WOMAN: Old Pops. Poor man. (BEAT) Now, I'm not saying you did something illegal with me, I'm just saying you did something illegal.

MAN: And that's what got us out there.

WOMAN: Yes, out there.

MAN: And now…

WOMAN: We are back.

MAN: It seems so.

WOMAN: We are. Bags in the trunk and everything.

MAN: Eating and drinking here, like we used to.

WOMAN: Like we once did.

MAN: Feels nice.

WOMAN: (BEAT) aren't we too old for this?

MAN: No, on the contrary, we are-

WOMAN: Old enough.

MAN: Old enough.

SOUNDS OF KISSES AND LAUGHTER

WOMAN: (PAUSE) it's not as cold as I thought it would be.

MAN: That's good, wouldn't want you to catch something.

WOMAN: Is it how you imagined it?

MAN: Wrap that scarf around you more, woman.

WOMAN: I'm not cold.

MAN: You could be soon.

WOMAN: Is it?

MAN: Hm?

WOMAN: This, is it how you thought it would be?

MAN: I'm not sure I thought it would be anything.

WOMAN: You must have thought sometimes.

MAN: I doubt it. The scarf, tighter please.

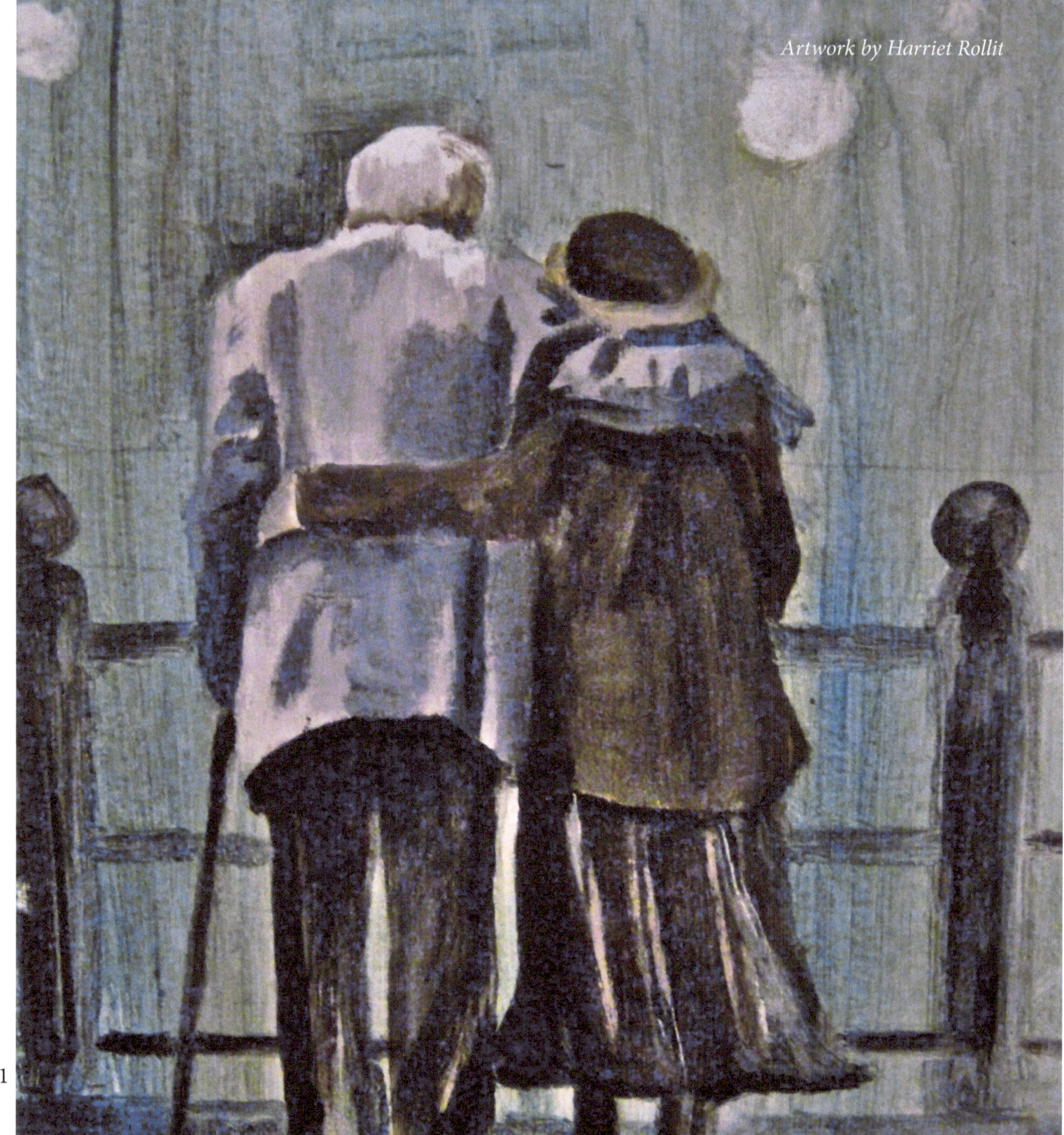

Artwork by Harriet Rollit

31

WOMAN:	Did you miss it?
MAN:	I don't think I did.
WOMAN:	Did I? I wonder…
MAN:	Put this hat on too.
WOMAN:	I'll look ridiculous!
MAN:	It will keep you warm.
WOMAN:	Fine, alright.
MAN:	Now that's a good girl.
WOMAN:	A good old woman, you mean.
MAN:	A good old enough girl.

SOUND OF KISS

WOMAN:	I honestly thought you would miss it.
MAN:	Got nothing to miss here; took it all with me when we left.
WOMAN:	A suitcase half empty with clothes you threw away first chance…expect for this hat.
MAN:	And that scarf.
WOMAN:	You would miss none!
MAN:	I took you. (BEAT) I miss you.
WOMAN:	I'm still here, Tom.

MAN: Yes.

WOMAN: It's not time yet.

MAN: They said he'll see you first thing tomorrow morning.

WOMAN: (PAUSE) This thing smells like an old man.

MAN: It will do its purpose. Leave it on. I don't smell that bad, do I?

WOMAN: All these years, you could have gotten a new scarf.

MAN: I like this one. After we settle in the hotel, let's go take a walk and see what else has changed.

WOMAN: You can afford a new one.

MAN: We have plenty of time to kill today.

WOMAN: Let's buy one.

MAN: I'm keeping this one. You made it. (PAUSE) Annie, he's the best.

WOMAN: That's what they all say.

MAN: We have nothing to lose.

WOMAN: You could lose me.

MAN: Let's cross that bridge when we come to it.

WOMAN: It's going to happen.

MAN: It's not happening now. And look, we are even back here!

WOMAN:	We are old enough to be back, you say.
MAN:	Yes, old enough. Let's get you to a warm place; it's starting to get chilly.
WOMAN:	I'm not cold.
MAN:	You'll be warm there. We'll get a proper dinner in your stomach.
WOMAN:	It's been months since I managed a proper dinner, Tom.
MAN:	Time to change that. Now that we are back, let's celebrate it with a big, unhealthy one!
WOMAN:	(PAUSE) Why are we here? Why are we, really?
MAN:	He's the best, Annie. We are lucky he's agreed to see us.
WOMAN:	Why did you bring me here?
MAN:	I wanted to…I still have…
WOMAN:	Hm?
MAN:	What's that word?

BLACKOUT

About The Piece
'This piece came about as a collaboration to Project Fifty. We were giving a word to write about, and this is what came of mine. Can you guess it?'

About Sherezade
She's doing an MA in Creative Writing and editing this magazine. Currently she spends her time editing mags, reading and applying for PhDs.

Excuse Me While I Put You On This Pedestal

William Sebag-Montefiore

I've already created you
And been with you a thousand times,
I've already held your hand
And we've already said these lines.

I've already stroked your hair
And massaged your aching back,
I've already kissed your forehead
And seen how you react.

I've already adored your eyes
And lost myself inside them,
I've already touched your beauty spots
And the temples that lie beside them.

I've already made love to you
And nestled in your covers,
I've already been bestfriends with you
And the most intimate of lovers.

I've already thought all this through
And planned every bit out,
I've already lost faith in you
And wrestled with my doubt.

I've already told you how unique you are
And how in awe I am of you,
I've already cooked you many meals
And even a desert or two.

I've already written you thirty poems
And recited them out loud,
I've already found in you my home
And gold lined sacred cloud.

I've already fallen in love with you
And know exactly how I feel,
But I'd like to find out what you think
And try it out for real.

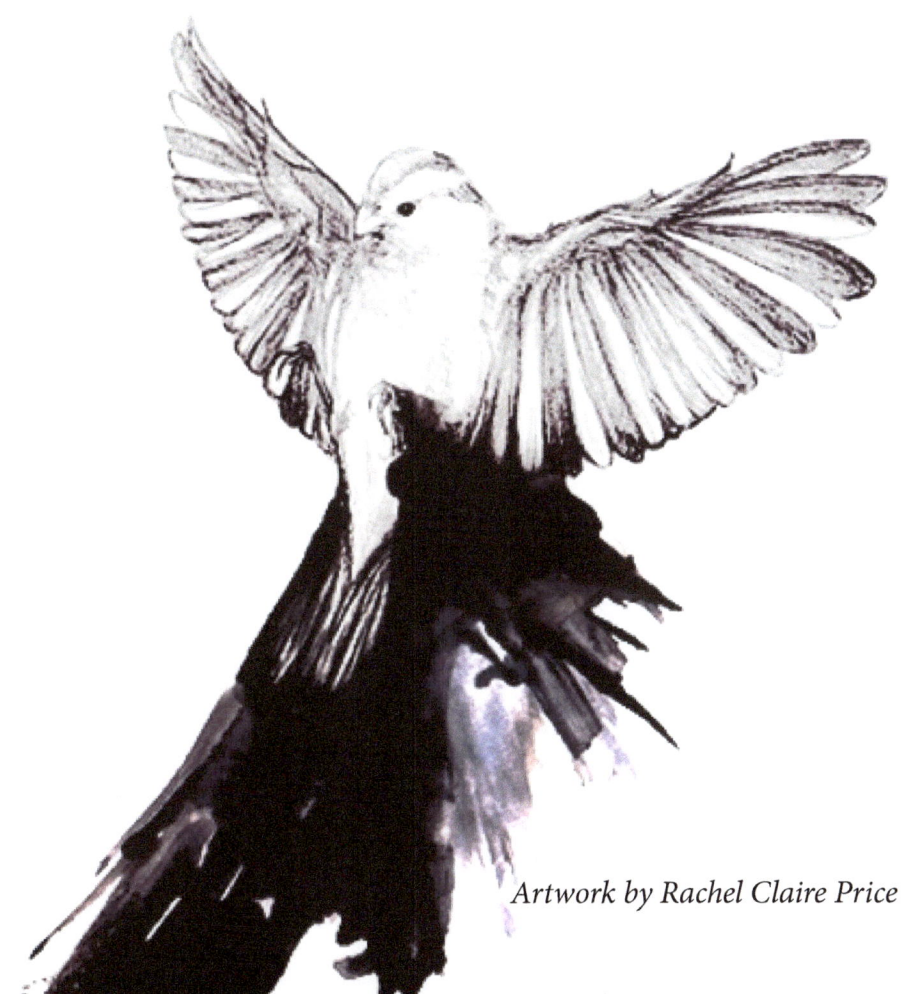

Artwork by Rachel Claire Price

Ode: Aberrations of Immortality

Andrew Sclater

Hiawatha, that long superior fellow
in feathers shakes his spear
at the diggers founding Tesco
in a corner of Co. Sligo
Innisfree a little longer

but under attack like J. Kerouac
eating chocolates with his mother
in some clapper board shack
in some broken Adirondack
chair or other.

In the Leaves of Grass
the Lady of the Lake
meets Childe Harold. He makes a pass
while Alice smashes plexiglass
for Fuck's sake

into Gunter Grass and Ginsberg's petty
squabble over Frank O'Hara's
lunch table. Mines a Ferlinghetti
bolognaise. Dante Gabriel Rosetti
sings a sea shanty and drinks amara

on a mat on a pier
in the withering sedge of the lake
in a Turkish hat. The time is near
for mirth and song and beer.
Amnesia to William Blake!

Rake out your poems' lurking prions!
In Ted Hughes' shoes, a Martian ices
buns with spoons of Muldoon's zwitterions.
This jar of candied peel was Sean O'Brien's!
Here's Marvell milk for Colette Bryce's custard slices…

Sobering up on a way through a wood
I come across Robert Frost
and ask which of the paths I should
take to find a real good
way of getting lost

(since Dryden is riding behind us,
Gray stands stuck in the graveside earth,
and Lord Byron fires blanks to remind us
to pay a groat to the organ grinders
who struggle to give birth -
though they never will -
to the golden daffodil).

Frost asks if I might raise the fee
to pay for such advice,
until he thus confronted me
I'd though he was quite nice.

Thus, from fear of mental congestion
I tend now to avoid the question…
although Edgar Poe should know,
as Sylvia Plath gets out the bath,
how Donne 'scaped sun to oblivion.

Praise to these holiest in the height
for all is chaos in their light…
darkness comes when falls the night…

It's like they left their dirty underwear
all over my floor
and I picked it up and wore it.

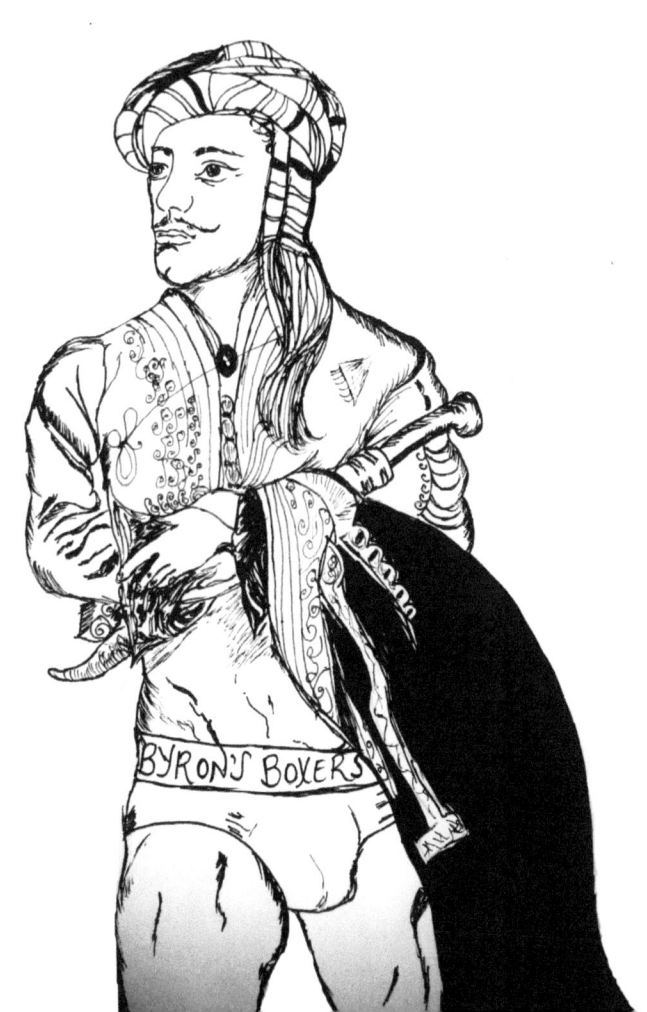

Artwork by Sophie Douglas.

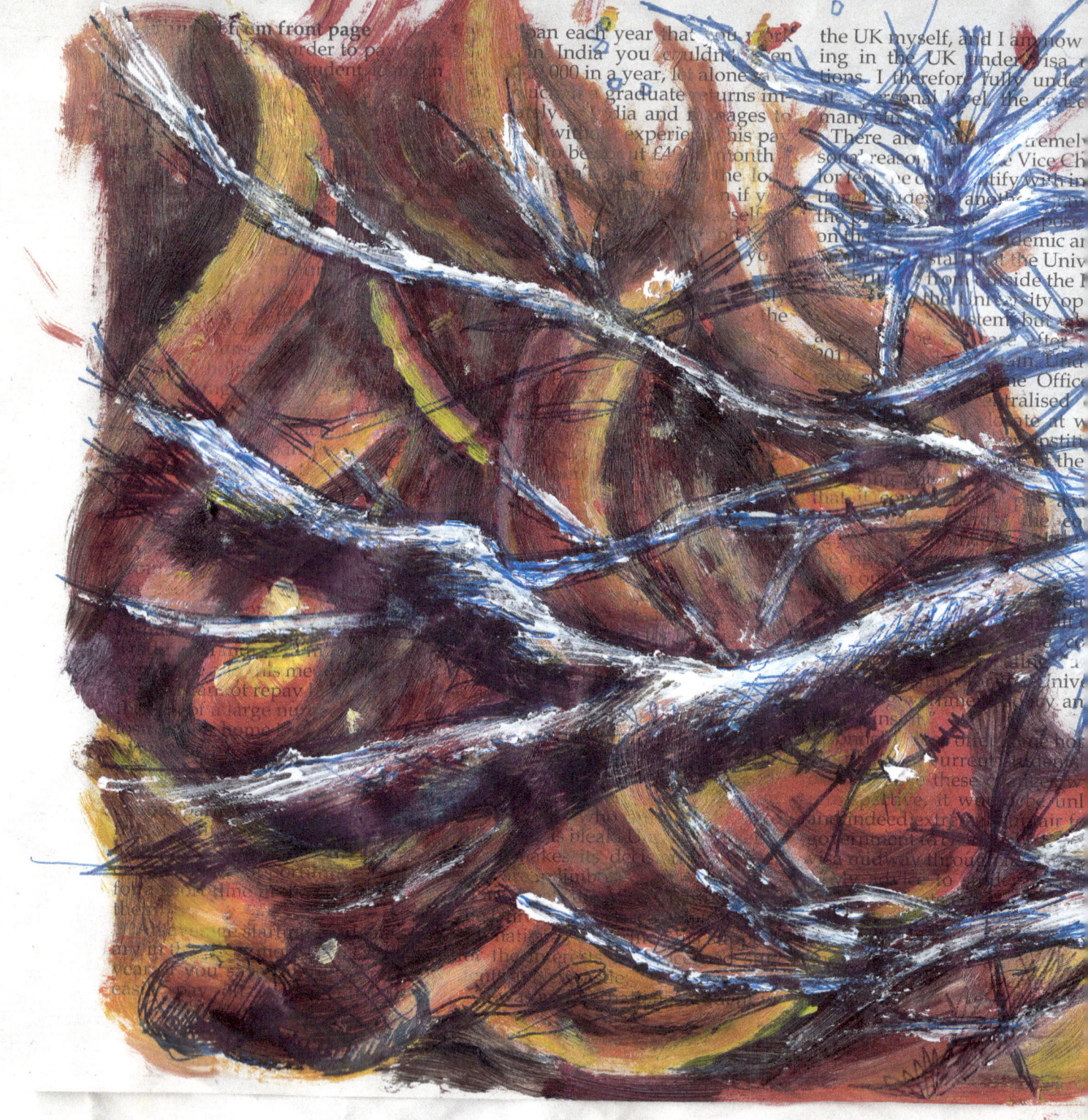

Artwork by: Katy Lawson

Arson

Laura Emerson

I am the firebug, or so they say,
and have been ever since the night
I took the glowing irons from the hearth
and seared my name into the clay.
The name remains upon the stones
and in my hand, a firebrand.

I've carried torches that have
cooled into old flames.
I've followed crests and flies into
their nests, high up in thorny branches,
gathered dry sticks below them,
brought them opals as offerings.

I've loaded ships with wood
and cast them loose, alight, to blaze
a trail of jewels across the night
and settle, singing, on distant shores.
I've caught the ash that falls, like stars,
upon my tinder tongue.

Inside this burnished box I keep
a flint and stone.
A rope, for kindling.
One lone match.

Heading Off

Tom Dibb

I passed a couple of old blokes the other day.
The sun was having his final check-round;
Making sure that he had remembered everything
Before he dashed off for a night's holiday somewhere different.

A guy in a wheelchair, ahead of me in the syrupy light,
And his mate beside him, ambling straight-backed –
Unhurried, it was as though they weren't moving at all,
But instead the world was simply rotating under their feet.

Shuffling along home – two pals sharing the afternoon path.
The wheelchair guy hit a bump as I strode past,
Tipping heavenward alarmingly, as if ready to go,
But his friend stuck out a steadying hand in time.

Nothing fancy. No grand emotion.
Just a pause, a chuckle, and then I was gone on ahead.
Yet the memory stayed with me as I strolled homeward;
The impression left by that hand there to check his fall.

Maybe somewhere down the line that'll be us,
Leisurely rolling to a halt together
With a hand ready to steady the other
And keep us side by side that little while longer.

I smiled as I thought of us stumbling into the finale together –
The sun pausing with his golden touch
To pat us on the shoulder like an old friend
Before heading off for a new day somewhere else.

About The Piece

'...it was actually something that happened as I was walking home from uni last year across the field by Castle Leazes. It seemed such a beautiful idea that the guy had so casually saved his friend from falling over backward onto the path and having a fairly serious accident, and it got me thinking about those relationships we have that aren't based on romance or attraction or anything like that – that are purely about two mates looking out for one another. I wanted the language of the poem to reflect the simplicity of the idea behind it so I deliberately steered clear of any potentially distracting abstractions or metaphors, and I'm happy with the cosy little poem it has become.'

About Tom

He grew up in a town called Bridlington on the coast (in East Yorkshire) with his parents, younger sister and two younger brothers. He attended Scarborough College from year 7 through to upper sixth before coming to Newcastle university to study English Lit (currently in his second year). He used to be a keen rugby player, but dislocating his shoulder a couple of years ago has meant that he's had to give that up. Unsurprisingly, rugby has been naturally replaced by an interest in poetry. He now splits his time between trying to get through the work for his course and taking full advantage of the Toon's student social scene - though the latter obviously takes up the majority of his energies. He also works part time as a carer for a local lad with autism, a job he finds hugely rewarding - in large part because his youngest brother is also autistic. When he writes he likes to draw on his own experiences for inspiration. He finds that poetry is most compelling and most effective when it is based in something real.

Amor

Eleni Makrygianni

Roar, my yellow wraith, you cannot be heard.
Bloom beneath the sunset; enchant my nights.
You are as morose as the heart of the earth.
The crooner of the lovers who murmurs in my ear…
'Amor is dead!'

Soar, my only friend, soar to the stars!
Lull me to a nightmare; awaken me in horror,
Shimmer, my pixie, underneath the vermeil moonlight.
Redeem the sufferers from all their sorrows;
Sing to them the words you speak to me:
'Amor is dead!'

Thereby, my friend, we shall all become your pets,
Your sympathy may quell our worries and our cries
And the loneliest ghosts of the mackerel sky shall defy this lie…
'Amor is Alive.'

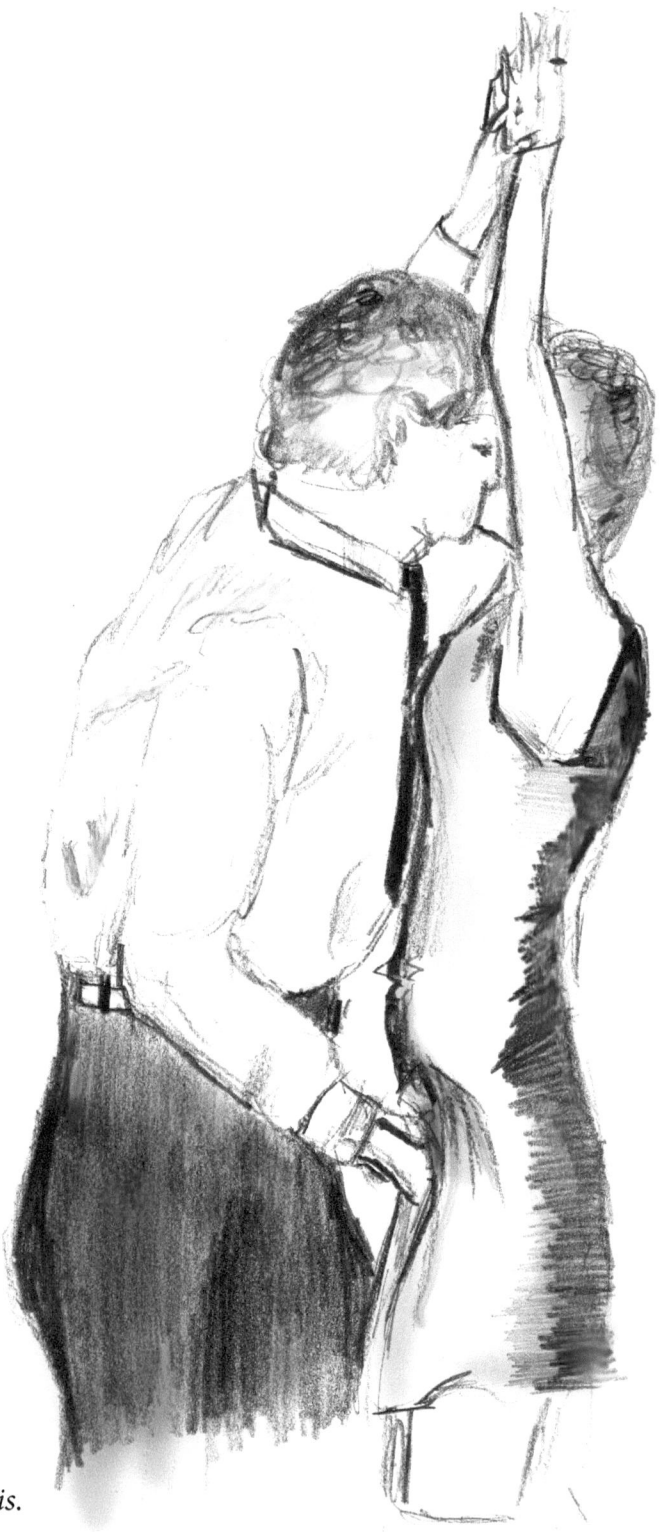

Artwork by Anthony Morris.

About The Piece

'Well, I was inspired by the obvious tragic loss of love and affection in our modern times. It all seems lustful and carnal when all we need is emotional purity. A higher connection, perhaps. Even the image of cupid has been deformed or even lost from my point of view. This poem perhaps depicts the nostalgia for romanticism.'

About Eleni

She's 2nd stage undergraduate student, BA Philosophical Studies, Newcastle Uni. Born in New York, raised in Athens, Greece. Age of 23. She has always found herself mingled with the arts. She's also volunteering for an art gallery in Newcastle. She loves writing even if sometimes words accentuate this sense of pressure and despair. Dreams : none, she lets time drive her wherever it wants.

Infatuated Youth

Tom Ward

When it's my turn to talk I've forgotten my lines
I've rehearsed them before alone, a thousand times
The words are wrong; this isn't what I meant to say,
Just filling the silence; leave it for another day.

Have another drink; it'll kill some time
The room is swaying, I can't make up my mind.
Why is no one else this way? I'm completely alone
Making a fool of myself I should've stayed at home.

You're as bad as me, but handling it better.
He's a lucky guy; I wish he'd not met her
Regrets in the morning when reality's dawning
It's happened again and we'll both pretend
The hidden meanings of our silent meetings,
3am thoughts and neither of us sleeping.
Our lives move apart, my chance was fleeting.

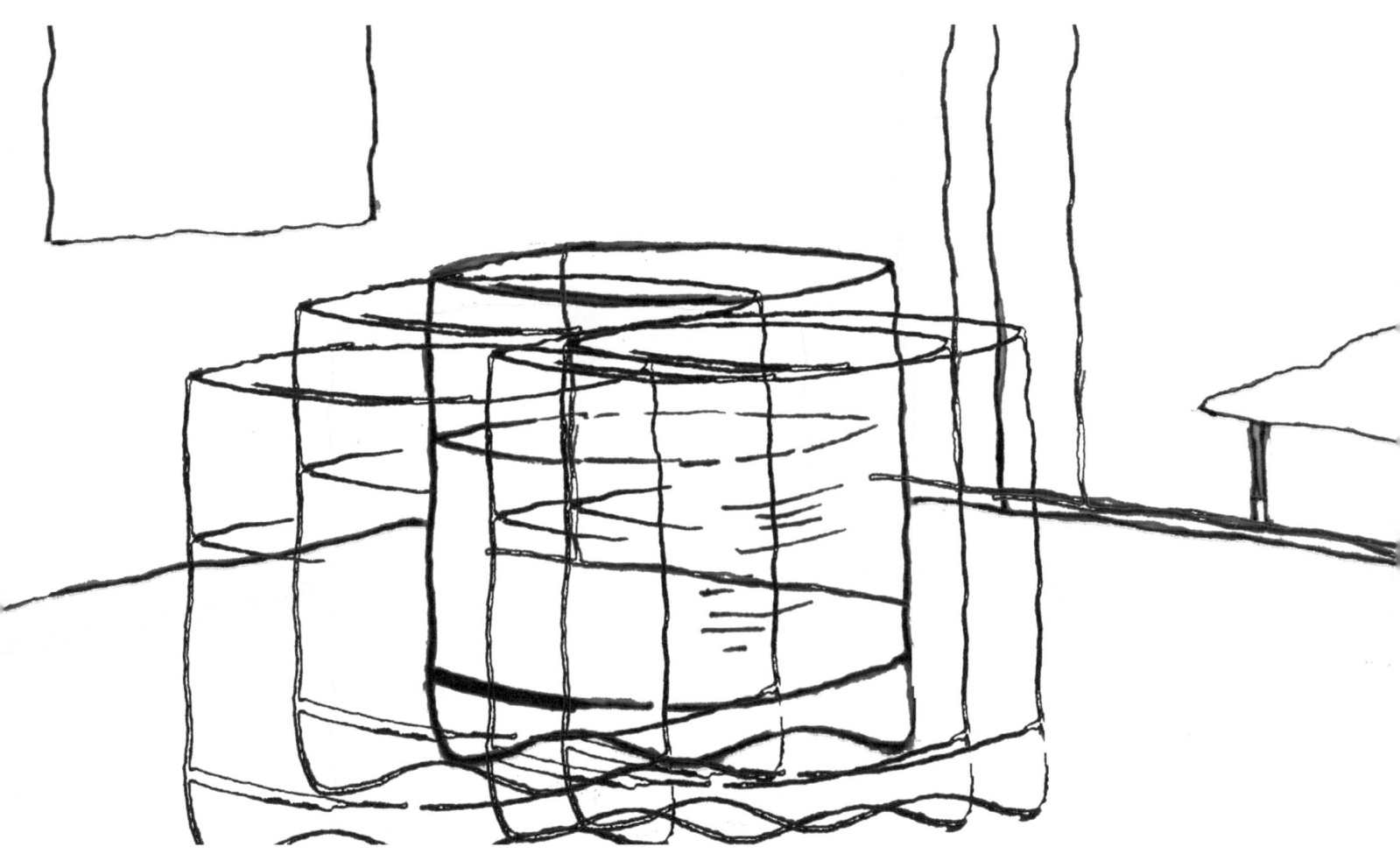

Artwork by Diana Afanador.

'They seek to work on the most basic of human emotions: Pity.'

-Margaret Thatcher, 1981

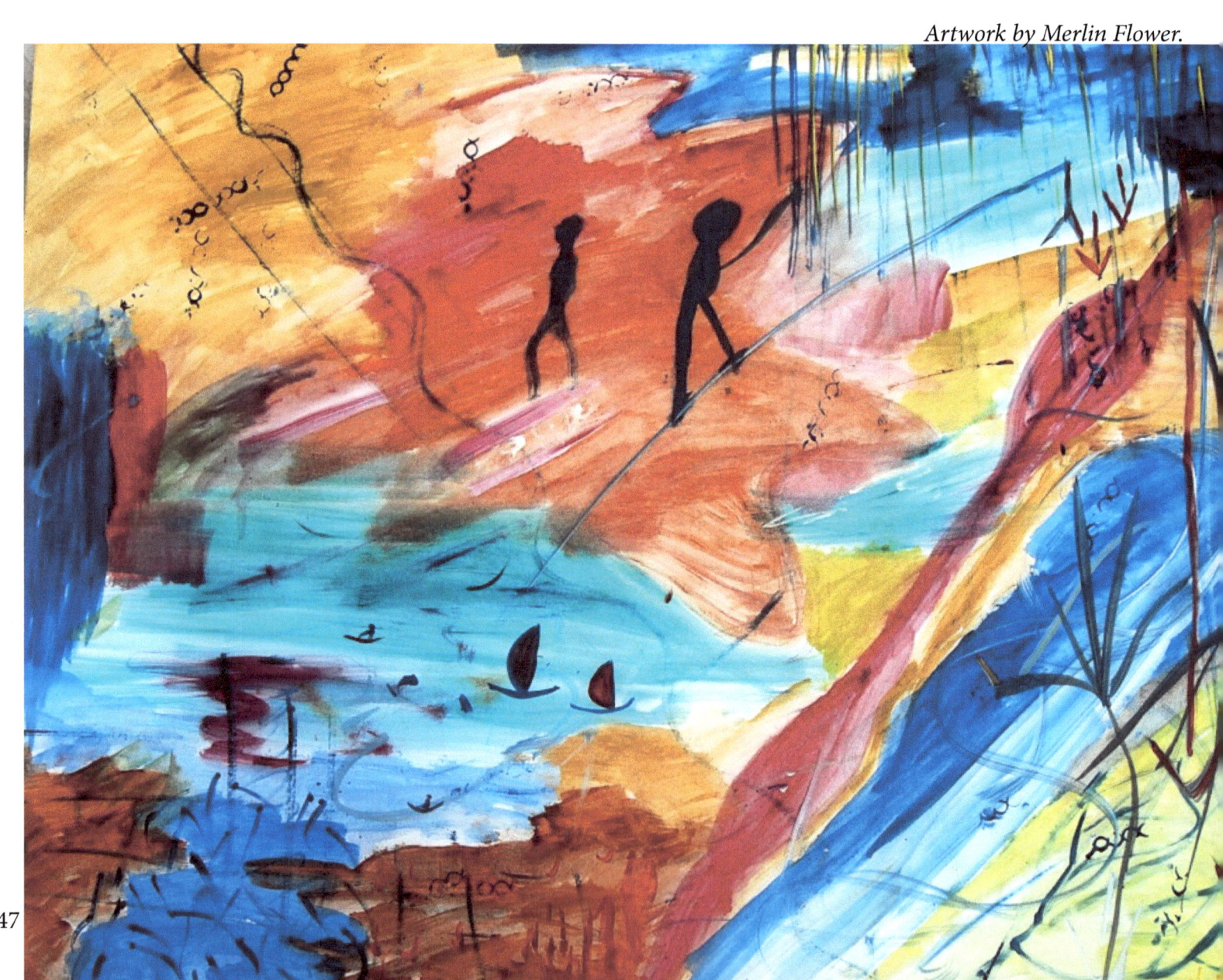

47

In the Eye of the Storm in a Teacup
Marcus Bryan

The Sun looks down through fog, but life goes on
Like yesterday; a heap of flesh and cloth
Remains unstirred by feathered wings and leathered feet,
The paper, tin, and ash that fall on concrete.
As Earth turns, indifferent, on its axis,
And shadow creeps across its surface,
Life departs the streets in all directions,
Each creature to itself, insensate.
Two spectres, alchemised within the dark,
Flit between the city's granite veins.
Steel glimmers, and blood obscures reflected stars
As screaming lungs are torn apart with blades.
Then silence. Bitter winds caress the figure lying
Barely breathing; choking, weeping, dying.
As the spectres vanish into misty dusk,
The Moon stares blankly at the Earth, as if to shrug.

About The Piece
'The poem was essentially borne out of watching too many science documentaries on the Discovery Channel and that really depressing Channel 4 documentary about the girl who got acid thrown in her face, the point being that if there's no God out there looking after each individual person, it gives a responsibility to humanity as a whole to not wear rose-tinted glasses about life.'

About Marcus
He's a 3rd year English student.

Her Charming Syllables

Daniel Ridley

You can't always start a new novel.
There is only a heart.

Worry, worry
I worried into a kiss
but look at us.
In all seriousness, this is rather good honey.

Strange and delirious,
untroubled for seconds;
both inappropriately ordered.

You had such a presence,
I could hardly look up.
You had such a presence,
I became bashful and relied on reticence.

There is a limited amount of time
in which to devote your life to sorrow.
I was tipsy but I remember.

I was tipsy:
April was outrageous.

Luminosity in a swept-left fringe,
I saw a fragment of a moment,
and held my drink with a limp wrist.

You stood making marionette impressions.
I caught your hair with my lips,
the day had taken ages.

I fought past your prologue,
and talked to you about the Beatitudes.

Previous nights were just dismal solutions
to the malaise of modern life
I only wanted a wife.

Of course,
retain your second name.
Protocol is guff.

There's now nothing without you.

I'm fretting dear,
which means I love you.

Artwork by: Remouse AKA
Russell Mountford

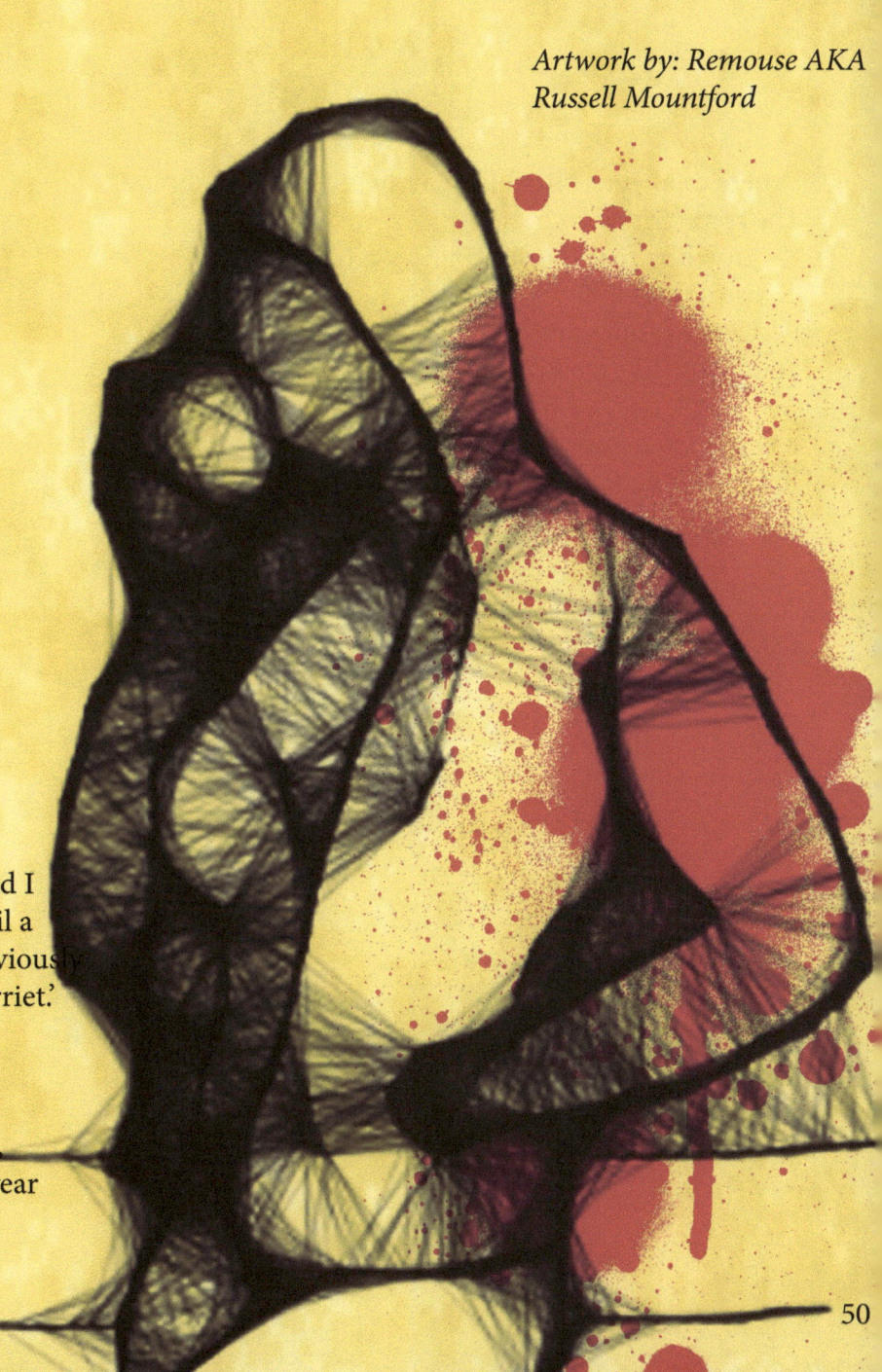

About The Piece
'The poem came from an immersion in Keats and I
suppose is about being desperately unhappy until a
chanced encounter frees you from what you previously
thought wouldn't ever end. It is dedicated to Harriet.'

About Daniel
He's a third year English Literature student. He
would love at some stage to own two bookshops,
one in Paris and one in Rome and spend half a year
at one and half a year at the other.

Love (or, A Parasitic Illness)

Sen Threadgold

Where does your blissful lodger lie?
The spiral iris of your eye?
Or grown as rose thorns 'round your heart,
Constricting, so it cannot start?
Perhaps within a cave-dark lung
Your lover, like a bat, is hung.

Such joy, to incubate and grow
Inside another's bone marrow.

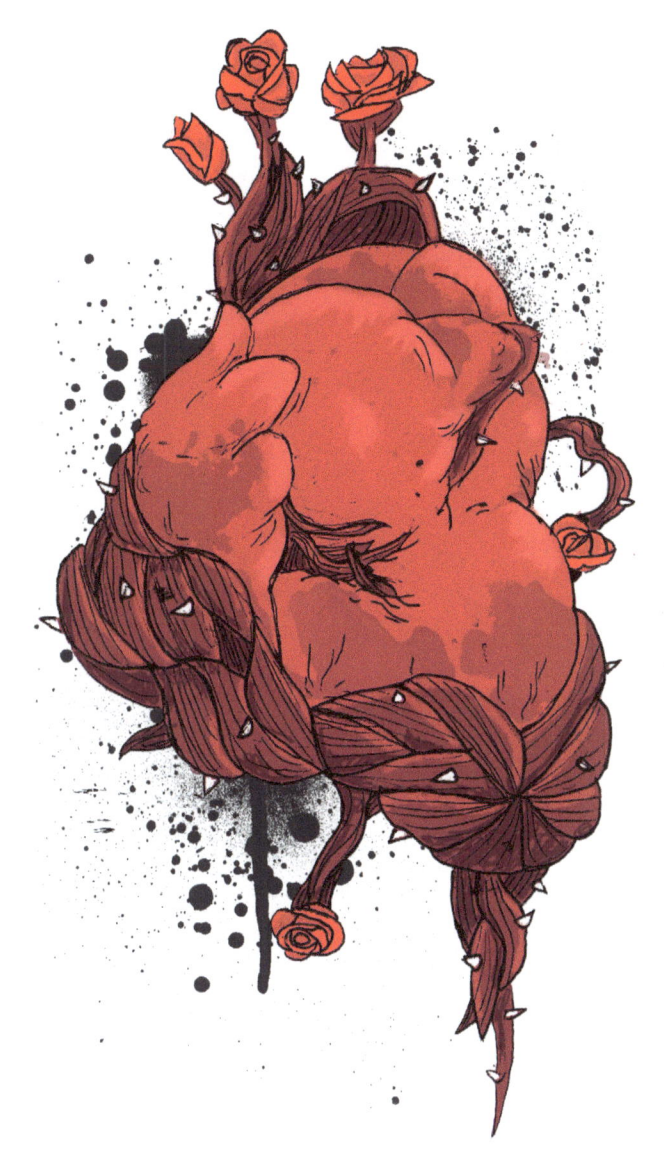

JOIN THE ALLITERATI

the best fresh talent in art and literature

alliteratimagazine.com

facebook.com/alliterati

Twitter@AlliteratiMag

www.ingramcontent.com/pod-product-compliance
Lightning Source LLC
Chambersburg PA
CBHW051051180526
45172CB00002B/597

9 781291 651911